Praise for

Tricks of the Trade to Success

"Paul Kelly has done it again! *Tricks of the Trade to Success* is a blueprint that pulls back the curtain on the magic behind Paul and his team becoming one of the largest and fastest-growing home-service businesses in America. Whether you're a small business, a Fortune 500 conglomerate, or just someone wanting to improve your life, you'll enjoy the simplicity and lessons inside."
—Calvin Merideth, Director of Sales—HVAC, Ferguson Enterprises

"Absolutely invaluable 'Tricks' for both business and personal success, written in an entertaining, enlightening, and digestible format. Paul Kelly is a 'roll up your sleeves' leader who pays attention to the details of how all things work, and to the psychology of what motivates people whether they be family members, employees, or customers. He incorporates all of this and more, revealing his *Ta-daaah* moments in chapters filled with his life experiences, business insights, and wisdom collected from others along the way."

—Viviane Essex, National Install Merchant, The Home Depot. 25-year veteran of the HVAC industry with extensive experience in sales, marketing, program development, and business management working with contractors, distributors, manufacturers, and retailers.

"I've known Paul for three decades and he's always been an enthusiastic learner. Here, after building a very successful business, Paul shares what he learned along the way in an easy-to-read book filled with helpful advice and useful tips for business and life."
—Spencer Lee, CEO, Roto-Rooter Group

"As a consultant, coach, and life-long learner, I'm always looking for insights into what drives a company or individual to rise to the top. This book gives valuable insight into the magic behind succeeding at the highest level. Get your *Ta-daaah* today!"

—Ron Smith, HVAC Legend, Crusader, Consultant, Coach, HVAC Hall of Fame Member, and author of the bestselling book *HVAC Spells Wealth*

"The philosophies that are the foundation of a successful business are the same ones that drive a winning sports team. I really enjoyed this book and I encourage everyone to experience the magic that it will bring to you personally, for your business or passion. GO IRISH!"

—Daniel Eugene "Rudy" Ruettiger, motivational speaker, author, and inspiration for the film *Rudy*.

"Paul's ruthless pursuit of simplicity with very complex issues is refreshing! He tackles our industry's biggest problems with straight-forward solutions, great stories, and a little bit of magic. Paul has a clever and witty way of helping you learn important lessons through simple but powerful words of wisdom and experience. He brings meaning to life's moments that most would normally never notice, and he turns them into valuable lessons for success in work, business, and life. I can't tell you how many times this book made me nod in agreement, smile, even laugh out loud. Paul's passion and respect for the service industry is unparalleled."

—Mike Hart, Vice President of Sales, Lennox Industries

"Paul Kelly has written a comprehensive, practical, personal, and at times humorous narrative of the realities of growing a home-services contracting business, with the theme of magic as its foundation. He has seen it all and made it happen, and throughout this book he adds insight into the hard numbers of contracting, as well as a variety of unique, personal anecdotes to emphasize the importance that family and the lessons of life can have on business development. It's a must-have for any business owner's library."

—Terry McIver, editor-in-chief, *Contracting Business*

"If we can learn the tricks that Paul Kelly so generously shares, perhaps we, too, can magically become motivational leaders and community icons. He has built a reputation of integrity, philanthropy, and compassion, an obvious reflection of the values and lifelong lessons that he shares in this book."

—Derrick M. Hall, President & CEO, Arizona Diamondbacks

"*Tricks of the Trade to Success* is a must-read book for any home-services business leader who is truly serious about sustaining or accelerating growth. I have been in this industry for nearly four decades and this book is absolutely among the best I've read. Paul does a masterful job of providing practical how-to advice, supported by how he has achieved industry-leading results."

—Mike Bidwell, President & CEO, Neighborly
(the world's largest home-service franchisor)

"If you are ready to transform your contracting business, then put this book at the top of your reading list. It's not by chance that Paul Kelly's career is full of *Ta-daaah* moments. Let the master magician show how you, too, can create and motivate your team to do a lot of little things consistently better than the competition does them.

—Bruce Matulich, CEO, EGIA (a nonprofit, industry-leading training organization helping contractors achieve success)

"I've witnessed many of Paul's *Ta-daaah* moments first-hand and this book is one of his best. The core philosophies and ingredients of success that have helped Paul, his team, and others perform at extraordinary levels are truly magic. His simplified approach to solving the complicated challenges we all face is refreshing. This is a must-read for any entrepreneur, leader, manager, or anyone who aspires to be more successful."

—Ken Haines, CEO, the Wrench Group, a national leader in home-repair, replacement, and maintenance services

TRICKS of the Trade to SUCCESS

THE MAGIC OF CREATING YOUR
TA-DAAAH!
IN BUSINESS AND IN LIFE

PAUL KELLY
FOREWORD BY MARK MATTESON

KING OF THE CASTLE PUBLISHING

Published by **King of the Castle Publishing,** Phoenix, AZ

ISBN 978-0-578-31494-5

Designed and printed in the United States of America

Contents

Foreword

I HEARD ABOUT HIM LONG BEFORE WE MET. At an industry conference, several influential leaders I respect said to me, "You need to meet Paul Kelly from Phoenix, Arizona." We bumped into each other on the last day, after I delivered the closing keynote and we hit it off immediately. I asked him to be a guest on my podcast. He graciously agreed.

Paul is impossible not to like. He reminds me of Ron Howard, one of the most influential and successful directors in Hollywood. Mr. Howard's films are always critically acclaimed and wildly successful at the box office—yet when you watch an interview with him, he is affable, humble, kind, empathetic, and openly shares his secrets to success. It's obvious he's the smartest guy in the room. Paul Kelly is like that, too. He is an open book. He will share his insights and words of wisdom with anyone who asks. Contractors seek him out because he has built one the finest and most successful home-services businesses in the world, growing twenty to thirty percent every year since 2004 when he purchased Parker and Sons in Phoenix. He has attracted the very best people in the region and created a culture of peak performance and profitability.

Paul is a true Level 5 Leader—humble, kind, well-spoken, quick to give credit to his team, and the first to use self-effacing humor to lighten the mood in a room full of stars. The book you're about to read—his first—is filled with hard-earned business lessons, but written in Paul's authentic voice and composed of short, easily digested chapters. Paul uses magic as the metaphor to solve the most perplexing and difficult challenges business owners face (like attracting, finding, and hiring the best people), and offers up simple (not easy!) solutions to improving morale, profitability, and peace of mind. Reading this amazing book is like sharing a meal with a world-class magician as he pulls back the curtain to expose how the illusion is done. Books like this are meant to be studied six or seven times, and you will go from tragic to magic if you study it with pen in hand. It will, if you are teachable and willing to apply Paul's proven principles, change your business and life in ways you can't even imagine.

I have worked with some the largest and most successful contractors in the world. Paul Kelly stands at the top of that hill. The world needs more people like him and I'm proud to call him my friend. He walks his talk. He is the cool breeze in a world filled with stuffy rooms. Buy this book. study it. Apply its principles. Then invest in copies for your employees. You'll be glad you did.

Aren't you worth it? I think so. The best is yet to come. Just ask Paul Kelly . . .

—Mark Matteson, speaker and bestselling author

Prologue

ONCE UPON A TIME . . . there was an exceptionally odd magician, named Ernie the Magnificent, who performed the most bizarre magic anyone had ever seen. One night, while performing before a sold-out crowd, Ernie asked for a volunteer and chose Greg, a somewhat reluctant middle-aged man, to assist him on stage. The magician presented a sledgehammer and he and Greg took turns breaking things with it. Its authenticity was obvious to everyone.

With the sledgehammer firmly demonstrated as real, Ernie described the trick to the audience: "For my next trick, I am going to place my head on this table and Greg, our volunteer, is going to take this sledgehammer and hit me over the head with it."

You could hear the buzz of concern. Everyone was trying to figure out what this illusion would really be about.

Ernie slowly lowered his head, cheek to table. The anticipation mounted. With confidence and conviction, the magician shouted, "Go ahead. Give it a good swing and hit me over the head with it."

Greg, who was unenthusiastic to begin with, was now even more hesitant to participate. He kept thinking, *There must be a trick to this*. The audience was cheering by now, and the pressure to perform was mounting. Ernie glanced up, his head still pressed firmly on the table, and whispered to Greg, "Go ahead, it's okay." Greg, trusting the magician, raised the sledgehammer and, with one fluid motion, slammed it against Ernie's head. Ernie fell to the ground, unconscious. Security called an ambulance, which arrived shortly thereafter. They worked on Ernie for several minutes while the audience sat in silent disbelief. How could this trick have gone so wrong?

Ernie was taken to the nearest hospital. He flatlined twice and they had to revive him, saving his life. Over the next several weeks they performed numerous reconstructive surgeries on his face and skull and things were touch and go for Ernie.

Six months later, Ernie the Magnificent, the oddest magician ever, awakened from his injury-induced coma. His eyes opened wide, he sat up, he raised his arms high over his still-bandaged head, and yelled . . .

"TA-DAAAH!!!!!!!!!!!!!!!!!"

Really? **Ta-daaah?** (or *tada* for all you spell-checkers). Why **Ta-daaah** for Ernie, the oddest magician, or for this book, which is filled with lessons drawn from magic and the art of illusion? What do Ernie and this book have in common? Settle in, because you're in for a treat: We're about to discover the intersection of life and business, some magic for reaching your goals, and how to create and appreciate the **Ta-daaah** moments in your life.

So grab some popcorn, take a seat in the audience, and don't hesitate to raise your hand when the magician asks for a volunteer. It could change your life.

The lights are going down. The curtain is parting. The show is about to begin . . .

Chapter One

Create and Appreciate Your Ta-daaah! Moments . . .

What lies behind us and what lies before us are tiny matters compared to what lies within us.
—**Ralph Waldo Emerson**

Ta-da *is an enthusiastic interjection used when presenting or revealing something, especially to bring attention to it and produce excitement.* Ta-da *is informal and is often used to be a bit funny or silly. It is most commonly spelled* ta-da *or* ta-dah, *but it is often stylized to reflect how it is said, as in* ta-daaah! *When spoken, it is often accompanied by a gesture toward the thing being presented.*
—**Dictionary.com**

TA-DAAAH! IS NORMALLY SAID BY MAGICIANS, signifying the end of the trick and the moment that leaves the audience in awe, wondering how it was done. But what if you could use it throughout your life? What if you could say *Ta-daaah* and suddenly anything that you wished to accomplish would be done. Even better: you would know *how* it was done, the *secret* of the trick.

I've had many **Ta-daaah** moments, both personally and in business. Growing up and surviving as a member of a ten-person family in a three-bedroom house with five boys in one bedroom, three girls in another, and mom and dad in their own room (no fair!) wasn't easy, but Mom and Dad raised eight kids who all turned out great —a real **Ta-daaah** moment for my parents. Marrying Trisha, the love of my life, was certainly a **Ta-daaah** for me . . . although once in a great while I think Trisha might describe it as a **Na-daaah** (as in "nada"), but being married for thirty-seven wonderful years is quite an accomplishment and something we're both proud of. We have two exceptional kids, Josh and Justine, who are definitely **Ta-daaahs.** I couldn't be prouder of what they've accomplished and, even more so, who they've become. Probably more a credit to their mom than to me, but this is my book and I'll still claim them as a **Ta-daaah**. We'll talk about them later.

I loved magic when I was a kid. I enjoyed watching it, learning about it, and trying to figure out the secrets of the tricks. In my early forties I stumbled upon a local community college's summer class schedule in the community paper, and there it was: *Magic for Beginners*. I always wanted to learn, so why not? I showed up for the first class. A local magician was the teacher and there were seven students, three of them under the age of twelve, a couple teens, a twenty-something . . . and me. I felt like Kramer from *Seinfeld* at the dojo with a bunch of kids. This probably wasn't going to be a good fit for me.

But I stuck with it. We learned a couple tricks in the first class, was told to go home and practice, and then performed them in the second class. Then we learned another trick and went home to practice that one. This was the pattern of the course and the tricks were very basic, though still very effective. When done well, these tricks could astonish anyone, even forty-year-old grown-ups. What the class did for me was force me to start learning magic, and in that process, I got even more into it. I stayed after class one day to talk to the teacher, a very talented magician, and I talked him into giving me private lessons at his house. We made a deal: He'd teach me two complex tricks, I'd practice them for three or four weeks, then I'd perform them for him. If he felt I was taking it seriously, and learning the tricks well, he'd show me another two tricks.

 Over the course of a year I learned about twenty tricks. His formula was simple:

1. Teach the student

2. Verify their understanding

3. Have the student perform to assess their skill level

4. Then, and *only* then, move on to a new batch of tricks

As great as the magic tricks were, it was this formula for learning that meant the most to me. I carried it into many aspects of my business and life, and it has helped lead me to the pinnacle of success.

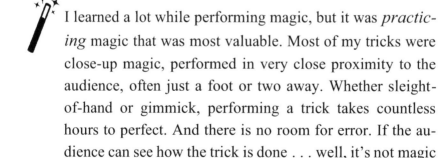 I learned a lot while performing magic, but it was *practicing* magic that was most valuable. Most of my tricks were close-up magic, performed in very close proximity to the audience, often just a foot or two away. Whether sleight-of-hand or gimmick, performing a trick takes countless hours to perfect. And there is no room for error. If the audience can see how the trick is done . . . well, it's not magic anymore, is it? Business, life, magic . . . they have a lot in common.

My biggest ***Ta-daaah*** was purchasing a relatively small HVAC (heating, ventilation, air conditioning) and plumbing company in Phoenix in 2004 and growing it from seven million dollars in gross revenue to a projected one hundred and ninety million in just seventeen years. All that growth was organic. With two recent acquisitions in late 2020, along with continued growth, we estimate we'll do over two hundred and fifteen million in 2021, and approach two hundred and fifty million by the end of 2022, all in one market. Is that magic or what? This growth will surely make us one of the largest, if not *the* largest, company of its kind in America in a single market, all in an industry where the average company size is less than a million dollars in revenue. Our biggest competitor is probably a quarter of our size and the one after that is maybe a fifth. We're in a class by ourselves.

I say it's my biggest ***Ta-daaah*** but it's really *our* ***Ta-daaah*** It took and continues to take a team, a group of people who are extraordinary at what they do and how they do it. Building a phenomenally successful company is our own little magic trick and I'm going to pull back the curtain and show you how we did it and how we continue to do it. And I think you'll be amazed by how simple the formula, concepts, and drivers really are. Notice I said they're *simple*, not *easy*. Nothing worthwhile is easy, but I have found simplicity is the key to massive success.

I pride myself on my ability to figure anything out. Give me a problem, especially one that no one else can solve, and I'll work until I come up with a real solution. Someone once challenged me with a problem that he swore I couldn't solve: how to live forever. I smugly dismissed the notion, not that I couldn't live forever, but that I couldn't figure out how to do it.

As I write this, I realize that I've finally figured it out. This book, and the lessons and concepts in it, once shared, are a form of immortality. I can live forever in the hearts and minds of my wife, kids, grandkids, great grandkids, and every generation thereafter; in the successes of other business owners, managers, supervisors, workers; to a mother, father, brother, sister, friend, or anyone who gets something out of this book that changes their life for the better. Hopefully I'll live forever in you, even if only in a small way. After all, we are the sum of everyone we've learned from or met, every book we've read, every movie or TV show we've watched, and every experience we've lived through, enjoyed, endured, or fought. We are a unique mix of our parents, our teachers, our relatives, our siblings, mentors, business partners, teachers, and even our pets.

Mark Matteson, one of my mentors and a very successful author himself (he wrote the bestseller *Freedom from Fear*), summed it up this way: "Writing a book makes you immortal." That's kind of neat to think about, that maybe one day, a hundred years from now, a great, great grandchild will be sitting under a tree reading this book. It's humbling. But more than that, it puts a lot of pressure on me to make this book a living legacy of what I've learned, what I know, what's made me successful, what's driven our business, and what I want to pass on to the world. That's an enormous responsibility and privilege, and a **Ta-daaah** that only you, the reader, can provide.

What **Ta-daaah** moments have you experienced? Maybe they were in sports or in school, maybe in some activity or skill you acquired. Maybe it was that perfect performance you couldn't be prouder of. Getting married? Your children? A promotion at work? Landing that perfect job? Buying or starting a business? A long-overdue divorce? Yes, even what might seem like a bad thing can end up being a *Ta-daaah* for you and for others. Death, for many, can be their final *Ta-daaah,* if you set yourself up for it to be that way (although there can be many more *Ta-daaahs* in heaven).

Ta-daaah is a mantra that ends a good trick, an act or effort, establishes how proud you are of what you just accomplished, and sets you up to perform your next performance. Hopefully this book will give you a few insights. More than anything, I want it to drive you to more success, both personally and professionally. Your *Ta-daaah* moment might be just a sentence or a chapter away. It might be right around the corner with every decision you make. Be proud of what you've accomplished: Your *Ta-daaahs* are all yours. No one can take them away from you. And one *Ta-daaah* can lead to many more.

🎭 Pulling Back the Curtain

★   Teaching's only purpose is for the student to learn and to master the lesson. Verifying comprehension and mastering what was taught is the key. When you are the teacher, always have the student/employee practice and perform the skill you taught, before moving on to the next lesson.

★   We are the sum of everyone we've learned from or met, every book we've read, movie or TV show we've watched, and the experiences we've lived through, enjoyed, endured or fought. Make sure you fill your life with *quality* people, books, movies, and experiences.

My First Trick

Solve Any Ongoing or Repetitive Problem

IT'S ALWAYS A GOOD IDEA to start with one of your best tricks to capture the audience's attention, so I'm coming out early with one of my showstoppers. Don't worry, I have plenty of great tricks in the bag.

Here it is: I found a simple way to solve ANY problem, overcome ANY challenge, and fix ANY ongoing issue. And not just for your business, but for your personal life too. And if you think answers to difficult problems are complicated, you're going to love this simple two-step process. The trick to solving any ongoing or repetitive problem is . . .

Meet often enough
+ <u>With the right people</u>
= Solve any ongoing problem, challenge, or issue

Couldn't be simpler than that, could it? Meet often enough with the right people!

I discovered this simple way to attack ongoing, repetitive problems when I was confronted with the number-one across-the-board problem that plagues our entire industry: finding, hiring, and retaining great people. When I discovered this trick we were growing at thirty-plus-percent annually and hiring over a hundred people each year, many of them trained technicians and installers. We hire over twice that many now, so you can imagine how challenging this was then and still is today. Month after month, year after year, we struggled to achieve our staffing goals. Because of our extraordinary growth, we sometimes substituted quantity for quality, a compromise that I am never happy to make. I don't just want to add people, I want to add the *best* people.

Then it dawned on me: *What if* we grabbed all our department heads, committed to meet each week, and solve this hiring crisis together? *What if* we meet often enough, with the right people . . . What might happen? The answer became clear just a few weeks later.

 Why? Because I was determined that, unlike so many other meetings in so many other business settings, *our* meetings wouldn't waste everyone's time. We didn't meet every week just to sit there and stare at each other. We talked about our challenges. We came up with plans. We assigned responsibilities. And we held each other accountable for results. **A plan, assigning responsibility, and accountability**. Now there's a trio of game changers. In just a few weeks, we started seeing the fruits of our labor. We did things we'd never thought of before. We thought differently about the challenges. We called someone out when they agreed to get something done and didn't. That year, we met our staffing goals, grew over thirty percent, and solved our industry's number-one problem in our own business. We've been meeting every week since because, as successful as we are, it's still a challenge.

Alcoholic Anonymous (AA) uses the same formula. Meet often enough, with the right people, and you can beat the disease of alcoholism. In AA, you attend meetings as often or as little as you want. Some attend daily, most attend two or three times a week, others attend as needed, but your chances of success increase in proportion to your attendance. You share your challenges and learn from each other. There is a set plan (the twelve-step process), and everyone holds one another accountable. Meet often enough, with the right people, and you're on the road to recovery.

At WW (formerly Weight Watchers), regular meetings are also a crucial part of the success formula. Like beating alcoholism, losing weight is hard (just ask around) and it's more easily accomplished when you don't try to do it alone. A support group is your best chance of getting better results faster.

Meeting often enough with the right people, be they coaches, trainers, or support groups, will accelerate results in all kinds of endeavors or challenges in life and business. If the problems, the issues, and the challenges aren't being solved by this two-step process, ask yourself these two questions:

- Are we meeting *often* enough?
- Are we meeting with the *right* people?

Meeting often enough might mean meeting once or twice a day. It normally means meeting at least once a week. It rarely means meeting just once a month. That's normally not often enough.

Meeting with the right people normally means meeting with key people affected, or with those who are being prevented from achieving their goals. Getting good thinkers in your meetings is paramount. It might only involve people from within your company, but it can certainly mean bringing in some outside help—a trainer, a coach, a mentor, someone from your board, a vendor, a partner . . . maybe even a competitor.

This simple two-step method is primarily for ongoing issues that plague your business or your life. It's not normally for one-off problems or situational challenges like *Should we fire a problem employee?*, although meeting with the right person could still help you solve that.

When someone comes to me with an ongoing problem or a challenge and asks me to solve it, I ask them how often they are meeting and with whom. We then talk about which part of the formula is missing or falling short, and although I don't want to be invited to every meeting to solve every problem (I have other things to do!), if they can't solve the problem on their own I assure them that if they invite me we will solve it together. They rarely want me there, for no other reason than pride. They want the satisfaction and sense of accomplishment that comes with solving a difficult problem. They want to—and should be able to—solve their own ongoing problems, challenges, or issues.

This simple technique can be used to solve all sorts of things.

Personal	**Business**
Lose weight	Hire/retain great employees
Beat addictions	Double-digit revenue growth
Improve relationships	Improve marketing
Money issues	Gain market share
Health issues	Quality-control issues
Personal growth	Cost containment
Improve happiness	Safety issues
Become a better cook	Improve customer satisfaction
Train your pet	Logistics or delivery issues

And in today's fast-paced world, *meeting often enough with the right people* doesn't even have to happen in person. Virtual meetings via Zoom, Microsoft Teams, etc., can accelerate solving ongoing issues. It also simplifies getting outside help. It's harder to say no when you don't even have to leave your own living room. Phone conferencing works too, but there's something magical about seeing people eye-to-eye. You can have instant access to some of the best thinkers in the world in so many areas of expertise, and much of it is free for the asking (but be careful: FREE ongoing help and advice is sometimes worth exactly what you're paying).

So there you have it, one of the best tricks in my bag: Meet often enough with the right people to solve any ongoing problem, issue, or challenge. It's that simple . . .

Ta-daaah!!!!!!!!!!

Pulling Back the Curtain

★   Meeting often enough with the right people can help you solve any problem, challenge, or obstacle.

★   A good plan, assigning responsibility, and holding people accountable, *especially yourself,* are three key ingredients to success in any endeavor.

Chapter Two

The Butterfly Effect

Measure your success not by things you collect, but by lives you affect.
—**Joubert Botha**

*In chaos theory, the **butterfly effect** is the sensitive dependence on initial conditions in which a small change in one state of a deterministic nonlinear system can result in large differences in a later state.*

*The term butterfly effect is closely associated with the work of Edward Lorenz. It is derived from the metaphorical example of the details of a tornado (the exact time of formation, the exact path taken) being influenced by minor perturbations such as a distant butterfly flapping its wings several weeks earlier. Lorenz discovered the effect when he observed runs of his weather model with initial condition data that were rounded in a seemingly inconsequential manner. He noted that the weather model would fail to reproduce the results of runs with the unrounded initial condition data. **A very small change in initial conditions had created a significantly different outcome.***

—**Wikipedia**

I BECAME AWARE OF THE BUTTERFLY EFFECT WHEN MY MOTHER WAS DYING. My mom loved butterflies. For her, they were a symbol of so many things. They are beautiful, delicate, unique, and special. She felt the same about people.

But it's her personal qualities that I remember most:

- She made everyone feel special, put everyone else's needs before her own, and saw the good in everyone.
- Investing time and energy in family was her top priority. She loved talking about her family and listening to others talk about theirs. As she would remind us, *"Things don't matter, people do . . . and family are the most important people in your life."*
- She loved things to be clean and orderly. Running the vacuum when the carpet was already clean was a habit shared by all my siblings.
- She loved routines and had a system for everything (and I mean *everything*), from making a bed (you must do the hospital tuck), to what kind of glass makes your beer taste best. If you tried her system, you were sure to find out she was right: Beer does taste better and stay colder in a very small, thick, round glass. Cancer restricted her life in her last years, but she adjusted accordingly, developed new routines and systems, and found a new level of happiness with the hand that life had dealt her.
- She loved everyone equally. She had no favorites, and it was easy to see. If you challenged her to pick a favorite, and all of us tried many times, she would refuse. As she would say, *"You all are all my favorites. I love you all the same."*
- She never said bad things, never cussed. We all tried to get her to say a bad word once, and she tried, but she always stopped

herself, saying, *"I just can't do it."* People weren't heavy or fat, they were *healthy* or just *big boned.*

• And she was religious, attending mass every week, praying for others, and saying the rosary daily. But more than that, she lived her life in the Christian faith, following the teachings of the Bible, and trying to live her life as the Lord would want her to.

The greatest lesson we learned from my mom was *that everything matters . . . that everyone matters.* This is called the *butterfly effect,* the theory that the flap of a butterfly's wings on one end of the world could set in motion a series of events which could create a tornado on the other side of the world. In life, even the smallest change can produce a very large effect in someone's life and in the others around them.

We knew she loved butterflies, but as her time on Earth wound down it became evident that she would tell us, in her own way, what to learn from her life. My siblings and I saw many signs from her, most all involving butterflies, cementing the fact that she was already working with God to make us feel okay about it all.

During her last minutes, as I and all seven of my brothers and sisters gathered around her, we each told her the one trait that we admired most about her that, when incorporated into each of our lives, could have a dramatic effect on ourselves and others, and each of us promised to work on doing so. On October 22nd, 2016, at 1:48 a.m., as she took her last breath, the butterfly effect, orchestrated by Frances Kelly, through her children, was set in motion.

After my mom died, my sisters saw all kinds of butterfly signs. I won't go into all of them, but I will tell you about my own experience with one. I was playing golf with some buddies, just a couple weeks after she passed, and a butterfly followed me for an entire hole, from tee-off to green. I dismissed it, drove the cart to the next hole, teed off, hit my second shot on the green, and was ready to putt when the same butterfly landed on my ball . . . and stayed there. I watched it in awe for a maybe a minute, and then it flew away. I knew this was a sign from my mom, but more importantly thought, there's no way she's going to let me miss this birdy putt. I lined up the twelve-footer and wouldn't you know I missed it. What? I tapped in for par and chalked it up to Mom rooting for me but knowing this was something I needed to earn myself, another lesson she taught me.

About the strangest sign from the other side that I have ever witnessed, and which cemented me as a believer in the afterlife, was when my wife's dad died. Jim Sr. had struggled for so long and he was on dialysis for the last couple years of his life. He never complained about the cards dealt him, not once. He was someone who internalized a lot and overcame a lot with the help of his wife and kids. He struggled greatly during his last few days, and you could tell he wasn't going peacefully. This affected my wife, Trisha, greatly. At the layout for his funeral, with a packed house, a red cardinal showed up and started pecking at a window not far from the casket. This bird was almost annoying, he was tapping so much. It went on for maybe thirty minutes and then he was gone. Now coincidentally, my father-in-law was a bird watcher and lover of cardinals, so a sign from him in this way seemed appropriate.

The next morning, at the mass prior to his burial, this same bird, or one just like it, showed up and started pecking at the window again. This too lasted almost thirty minutes. This cardinal was so annoying, everyone was watching it, and everyone agreed that Grandpa was giving all of us a sign, and that he'd be annoying us for many more years to come.

Now the story would be incredible to me, and hopefully to you, if it ended there. But it doesn't. My wife and I flew home to Phoenix from the funeral in Cincinnati. The morning after we got home, in the master shower window, we heard a pecking at the window. My wife and I both jumped. We couldn't believe it. A red cardinal, like the one at the funeral, was pecking at our window in Arizona. That's a long flight for a bird. And it wasn't just that morning, but every morning for about three weeks. Thereafter it was sporadic, but once it even followed my wife from the bathroom window to the kitchen window, where it pecked at that window too. Whenever we tried to take a picture, it flew off. It was uncanny. This was Jim's way of telling my wife, Trisha, I'm okay now. Don't worry, I'm in a better place and I will never suffer again . . . but no pictures please.

After all those signs, I'm finally a converted believer in the afterlife and signs from your loved ones. Each sign was certainly a *Tadaaah* for those who had passed, and to me, my wife, and our family.

How does this concept apply to business? Should I be watching for signs from the afterlife to help steer me or my company to better results? *What is Paul getting at?*

The butterfly effect, put simply, means that small changes in your business, just like in life, can cause other changes, producing a very large and dramatic effect later. It means that everyone and everything matters. What you *do* matters. What you *say* matters. And sometimes a very small decision or change ends up producing a series of other changes and decisions which collectively lead to dramatic changes to your organization, family, or life.

 Deciding to write down your goals, or to even have *goals*, is exactly the kind of change that can lead to many life and business improvements. Deciding to be more *thankful* to co-workers, to your boss, to your company, although a small change, can produce an accelerating avalanche of positive results. Donating your time or money to a charity, even if in a very small way, can lead to others emulating your behavior, ultimately making a substantial and lasting difference. A small change to a creative advertising concept can produce substantial improvements in results. Getting just marginally better at something in your job can lead to other improvements which lead you to the promotion you always wanted. Not eating after 7 p.m., when you normally snack late at night, can lead to losing weight which leads to you eating better, which makes you healthier which leads to feeling better which leads to you working out which springboards you into training for a marathon which results in you meeting your future wife at the marathon event because she runs marathons too . . . You get the idea.

The list of small changes that lead to big changes is endless, and you never know what effects a small change will ultimately create. The future cause and effect of small improvements in your business or life are undeniable. Never underestimate the power of the butterfly effect in life or in business!

⚑ 𝒫ulling 𝒝ack the Curtain

★   Small, incremental, sometimes unnoticeable changes and improvements can cause significant progress and transformations. Never underestimate the power of positive change, no matter how minute or insignificant it may seem.

★   Everything matters. Everyone matters. What you say and do matters. Someone is always watching or learning from you. And if not on Earth, then up in Heaven. Make what matters something good.

★   Having goals, writing them down, and keeping them in front you at the wheel, will help steer you to success.

My Second Trick

How to Convince Anyone of Anything

I've been trying to convince my shadow that I'm someone worth following.
—**Rudy Francisco**

SOME TRICKS I'VE LEARNED FROM OTHERS. Some of them I've come up with myself. This one is all mine, and when I first performed it I just smiled. It worked! Then I tried it again and again, perfecting my delivery . . . and it worked again and again. I got so good at it, and it seemed so brilliant, I just had to share the secret of the trick with others.

Telling the secret of a trick is a big no-no for magicians, so I convinced myself it wasn't magic. I told it to enough people that some of them started trying the trick on *me*. Fortunately, I am keen to recognizing the ingredients of the trick.

How do you convince someone of something you want them to do, approve, or agree with?

Typically, the answer is to make them think it was *their* idea by steering the conversation until they come up with the answer you want on their own, a process that involves a long process of talking through the challenge or question until they reach the desired answer. Sometimes they get there. Sometimes they don't. Sometimes it requires hours of working this system. Sometimes it can take days or weeks to get them to come up with it. Sometimes they have to go through other answers first and even try some of them. It can be a long, hard, sometimes even delicate system . . . and sometimes it doesn't work.

Good news: I found a short cut.

How do you convince someone of any idea, even when you know they might not agree with it?

Pretend the idea was theirs to begin with.

Ingenious, isn't it? Just to be clear, this is not the same thing as trying to talk someone toward the desired conclusion. This is a similar idea, but with a different method, and you have to be a little crafty to pull it off.

1. What do you want to convince someone of? Fix it firmly in your mind.
2. Refer to a story or lesson that you learned from the other person. Embellish the details if you need to.
3. The lesson needs to be far enough in the past that it would be hard for the other person to remember it.
4. Give them credit for you learning the lesson from them.
5. Apply the lesson to the current thing you are trying to convince them of.
6. Thank them for the lesson.
7. Confirm the decision that you want them to agree upon.

24

All that might sound complicated, but it's not. Here's an example based on an actual circumstance: I wanted to give all the plumbers a raise because I felt the market had caught up to what we were paying our better plumbers. We always wanted to stay ahead of the market. My business partner, Vince, might be hesitant to give them raises. I needed to convince him. I said something like this:

"Vince, I was thinking last night about whether we should give raises to our plumbers, to make sure we stay ahead of the market . . . and I remembered something you told me a few years ago when we first met. You told me that if you want to end up with all the best plumbers, you have to stay ahead of the market and make sure they feel appreciated, and how we pay them is one way of doing that. And that if they feel appreciated, and you stay ahead of the market, they won't leave you. I thought about that and thought to myself, you know what, Vince is right. We need to give our plumbers a raise. I wanted to thank you for that. What do you think?"

Vince, of course, said, "You're damn right we need to give them a raise" 😊 .

This trick can work in your business or at home with your spouse or kids, your mom or dad, a sibling or a friend. If you happen to give this book to your spouse, make sure to rip this chapter out of it. We wouldn't want this secret weapon to fall into the wrong hands!

Here's another example, also a real-life one, of this trick in action:

About twelve years ago, my wife and I were looking for another home . . . our *dream* home. We set a budget, picked an area where we wanted to live, retained a realtor friend, and began our search. We weren't in a hurry, so we had time to find just the right house before we pulled the trigger. Over a handful of months we had gone through over fifteen homes. Now I like looking at houses, but it was starting to wear on me.

Then we found it: our dream home, in the area we wanted, with all the features and uniqueness we craved. It had a pool with a swim-up bar, a man cave grill and bar area, even a putting green. The interior was Tuscan style, with many upgrades, and was certainly one of a kind. The kitchen was huge, and my wife was thrilled with the open-concept floorplan. The finishes were top notch. I loved it. My wife loved it. The builder had built it for himself and his family, and unfortunately had to sell it during the 2009 real estate crash in Phoenix. There was only one problem: It exceeded our budget by over $100,000. We could afford it; it was just more money than we wanted to spend.

My wife wanted to pass on it because she's much more financially conservative than I am. I wanted to stretch and buy it. Trisha did not. She took the house out of the running and we were right back where we started.

So I used the trick.

"Honey . . . when we got married, over twenty-five years ago, I remember how hard you and I worked . . . and back then we couldn't afford nice things. We made enough to live on but we didn't have enough for luxuries. I remember you telling me, if we ever get in a position where we could live a better life, and could do it comfortably, you wanted to make sure we did it, *especially* when it came to our home. You said it's the one place we'll enjoy forever and where we can make memories with our kids. I always remembered that. This house is everything we ever wanted and, although it's a bit more than we want to spend, it's still within a budget we can afford.

It'll be the house we live in for the rest of our lives and our kids are going to love it. I want to thank you for all you've done to get us to this point where we can afford a house like this. How do you feel about it?"

Trisha said, "If you think we can afford it without strapping us, I think we should go for it."

I think you probably get the gist of the short-cut trick to convincing anyone of anything. It shouldn't be used all the time, but it can be used sparingly for important things. Convincing someone of anything is an extremely powerful tool and it can come with unintended consequences, especially if what you convince them of doesn't work out. Remember, this is something you really want bad. So make *sure* it works out!

Hopefully, convincing someone of something just got a lot easier by just pretending it was their idea to begin with.

Ta-daaah!!!!!!!!!!

ℙuꞁꞁing 𝔅ack the ℂurtain

★   Convincing someone of something can be as easy as pretending the idea was theirs to begin with. No one likes to argue with themselves.

★   The higher and longer your track record of success, the more influential or convincing you can be with others. Edward R. Murrow said, *"To be persuasive, you need to be believable. To be believable, you must be credible. To be credible, you must be truthful."* Be truthful and work on being successful in all you do. You will have *earned* the power of influence over others.

Chapter Three

My Biggest Ta-daaah!

The race is not always to the swift, nor the battle to the strong; but that is the way to bet.
—**Hugh E. Keough**

MY BIGGEST *TA-DAAAH* IS REALLY A WHOLE TEAM'S *TA-DAAAH*. I'm blessed with a bunch of team members who care as much about our company as I do. They do extraordinary things day-in and day-out. They are truly remarkable, and my story is really their story.

My business background started right out of college in auditing and then accounting. I became a CPA and eventually landed a job with Roto-Rooter, my entry into the home-services space. I eventually moved from accounting to marketing and then to operations, running a small Roto-Rooter location in Columbus, Ohio. From there I moved to Tampa to run a division for Service America, and then to Boca Raton to become VP of Sales. The CEO of Service America had left to start up a consolidation effort of HVAC and plumbing companies under the brand of Blue Dot, and eventually handpicked some of the Service America talent—including me—to help him.

I started with Blue Dot in 1999 as VP of the Western Region, responsible for acquisition input, performing due diligence, and most importantly, overseeing the companies purchased in the

Western Region. At one time, twenty-three companies were reporting to me. Blue Dot eventually was sold by their parent company, Northwestern Energy. At that time, Blue Dot had purchased over seventy-five companies in the HVAC and plumbing space and, instead of selling the whole package, Blue Dot sold it location by location, city by city. As it wound down, I had the chance to buy Phoenix in 2004.

Blue Dot's Phoenix location consisted of four acquisitions operating as three brands in the market: Parker & Sons, a two-and-a-half-million-dollar company focused on the west side of town, Environmental Conditioning, Inc (ECI), a three-million-dollar company focused on the east side of town, and Walter Anderson Plumbing, a one-million-dollar company. The fourth acquisition, Eskimo Air, was rolled into ECI. Combined, the group did seven million dollars in revenue.

I had a partner, Vince, who initially oversaw the Parker & Sons segment while I oversaw the ECI and Walter Anderson segment. I had known Vince since my days at Roto-Rooter and he was known as one of the best plumbing managers in the whole company. He taught me all about plumbing and how to gain a customer's confidence on the job. Vince knew how to win over customers until they were eating out of his hand.

Fast-forward a few years: Vince and I are both working at Blue Dot (I helped him get a job there). The Phoenix market for Blue Dot did seven million dollars a year, but its earnings before interest, taxes, depreciation, and amortization (AKA EBITDA, AKA *profit*) of forty-three thousand dollars. In spite of this, when Blue Dot began selling off their locations a bidding war developed over Phoenix. Vince and I were determined to own it, but with other determined bidders it was clear that we'd have to overpay. Now I was very familiar with how companies were valued, and normally it is a multiple of EBITDA. At the time, five to seven times the current EBITDA was a standard multiple for a well-developed company in a strong market. A multiple of EBITDA is certainly not how the Phoenix Blue Dot companies were valued though. When demand (buyers) exceeds supply (one group of companies in a market), price goes up significantly. We knew we could do great things in the Phoenix market and we were willing to pay for the chance to prove it. Unfortunately, so were a number of other would-be owners. We wound up paying seven figures for it. At the time, I was upset. We had paid too much. Today, I know that it was money well spent.

So, there we were, two partners with a combined revenue of seven million dollars and about thirty-five employees trying to do well enough to drive the business—at least enough to cover payroll and other bills, which was our primary goal during those first few months.

We quickly combined all four brands into one, as one of the classic mistakes some companies make is spreading their advertising and efforts over too many brands, diluting the effect that combined spending and efforts produces. Of the four brands, Parker & Sons seemed to be the most family-oriented name, although it was really only known in a small section of the west side of town. Vince became the face of our company and he played the role of "Grandpa Parker" in our ads. He was a true cowboy, so playing the part came easily for him. Vince, who had won the trust and love of his customers when he was with Roto-Rooter, was now doing the same in Phoenix with one crucial difference: He was now winning the trust and love of thousands of potential customers across the airwaves. He had that certain look and charisma, a sense of honesty, that you instantly recognize . . . and people took to him quickly.

Vince played "Grandpa Parker" in our commercials while over-seeing the plumbing department. I oversaw the HVAC department, as well as marketing, accounting, human resources (HR), warehouse, and all the other support functions. Our growth was slow at the beginning, but soon accelerated as we gained momentum. In 2003, the combined companies had done seven million dollars. In 2004, we did eight million. And then the accelerator kicked in, as we went from eight to eleven to seventeen to twenty-three million dollars. We started growing by five to seven million each year—the size of our company when we bought it. The last few years we've been able to grow twenty to twenty-five million, and this past year, the year of COVID-19 and all that brought to upon us, we grew a whopping thirty million dollars. That's the size of our second-largest competitor in Phoenix.

At this writing, we are tracking toward another strong growth year of thirty-million-plus and should do close to a hundred and ninety million in total revenue. That's all-organic growth, meaning there were no acquisitions which contributed to it. It all came internally, from marketing, advertising, referrals, improvements in close rates and average tickets, from price increases, and from adding other services. The growth came from hiring exceptional managers and leaders, including a gentleman by the name of Daryl, probably one of the brightest leaders in our industry. After hiring Daryl, who is now our president, we started growing fifteen to thirty million dollars a year. We recently bought two more companies in town which we will combine into another brand in the market, separate from Parker & Sons, bringing our combined revenue, just in Phoenix, to nearly two hundred and twenty million dollars in 2021.

Oh, I forgot to mention . . . I sold the company back in 2015. Talk about a *Ta-daaah* on top of a *Ta-daaah!* Vince had been winding down and wanted to retire back in 2014, so I bought him out. A year later I sold it to a private-equity group called the Wrench Group, the leader in the home-services consolidation effort, that put together four companies in the HVAC, plumbing, and electrical space. We've grown a lot since then and currently have locations in Arizona, California, Colorado, Florida, Georgia, Indiana, Kentucky, Maryland, Ohio, and Texas. Leonard Green & Partners (LGP), a leader in their space, is the investment group that helps to support our efforts, both financially and directionally. They are an awesome partner and provide great support while still understanding the autonomy needed to be successful. Ken, Wrench Group's CEO, and Paul, their COO, steer the ship masterfully, avoiding the painful mistakes endured by other consolidators over the years. We're building a better mousetrap in our industry, on our way to being a one-billion-dollar company within the next two years.

Ta-daaah!!!

 ## Pulling Back the Curtain

★   Some companies or leaders spend a lot of time looking over their shoulders at their competition. Like a world-class sprinter or swimmer, I always believed in keeping your head down, running your own race, and competing against yourself or your last personal best. Worrying about what someone else is doing usually slows you down.

★   Partnering with "best in class" organizations elevates your game. You will never do it alone, so why not partner with the best? As John Kennedy said, *"A rising tide raises all boats."*

Chapter Four

Interesting Facts About Parker & Sons

The impossible is justified by the fact that it occurred.
—**Honoré de Balzac**

YOU PROBABLY DON'T WORK FOR PARKER & SONS, but when a company has enjoyed the kind of spectacular growth that ours has it pays to look back at what drove it. The concepts and ideas in this book are the key ingredients of what went into our recipe, and among the results are some interesting facts . . .

• Every day, our four hundred and thirty vehicles travel about twenty-six thousand miles, a little over a thousand miles more than the circumference of the planet, so our vans and trucks, collectively, drive around the world every day. Just imagine the size of our gas bill.

• On our busiest day last year, when it was a one hundred and sixteen degrees in Phoenix, we took over four thousand incoming calls. Hats off to our inbound and outbound call center, and the many others who jumped in to help.

• Our field technicians, installers, and supervisors, have over three thousand years of collective experience. Sounds impressive, but it just means we know how to manipulate numbers to our advantage. Our average experience level is around eight years, which is long enough to know that you don't want to do this kind of field work when you're sixty.

- Despite our size, doing over two hundred million in revenue with two recent acquisitions, we only have about a nine-percent market share in Phoenix. That means that nine out of ten consumers aren't using us. We have a long way to go to claim dominance. Right now, our industry is dominated by small one-to-three truck operations. It's highly fragmented and the barrier to entry is low.

- The U.S. home service industry is a six-hundred-plus billion-dollar industry and growing. That's about half of just one congressional stimulus package during COVID-19. Everything is relative.

- Our next biggest competitor in Phoenix is a quarter of our size. The next after that is a fifth of our size. We've really distanced ourselves from the competition over the last five years.

- Between TV and radio, we run seventy-five thousand ads a year. That's an average of over two hundred spots a day, or close to nine per hour, or .15 spot per minute. Just because you can break something down to the ridiculous doesn't mean you should ☺.

- Our employees (field and office), on average, make thirty percent more than the market normally pays for similar positions. And yes, they are worth every penny!!!!

- We have three full-time auto mechanics who do extraordinary things to keep our four hundred and thirty vans on the road. Our lead mechanic was one of the first to work on driverless cars. One of our technicians once parked on a hill and forgot to put his van in park. As he walked away, the van took off down the street. Okay, so that's not what I meant by driverless technology, and that didn't really happen, but when I say our mechanics do extraordinary things to keep us rolling it's the absolute truth.

Chapter Five

Spend Wisely

Yesterday is a cancelled check; tomorrow is a promissory note; today is the only cash you have, . . . so spend it wisely.
—**Kay Lyons**

I LEARNED A LOT FROM MY DAD, but one of the most profound lessons was how to spend wisely. And not just money, but time and energy or effort as well. I'll use energy and effort interchangeably throughout the chapter. He didn't make a lot, and he certainly hadn't saved much. Raising and supporting eight kids on what he made was a form of magic and I'm still trying to figure it out. When I got old enough, I knew exactly what he made because I did my parent's tax returns. Shortly after college I was making more than he did . . . and trust me, it wasn't much.

My dad worked for the local utility company, Cincinnati Gas & Electric, and fixed and cleaned furnaces on the side for extra money. He worked up to sixty-hour weeks normally, but during the winter he could work over seventy hours, pulling double shifts. We only took one big vacation and that was to the Smoky Mountains. He saved up awhile for that one. Other than that, our biggest treat was a trip to Coney Island (the one in Cincinnati) every few years. When my parents bought groceries, they didn't buy food that everyone liked, they bought food they thought would last the longest. If we didn't like the cookies, then they'd last a lot longer than our favorites would. Money was tight, and Dad watched how he spent it very closely.

When you work a lot, your free time is scarce. Having eight kids, most of us in sports, means there are games and practices to attend. As scarce as his time was, he was always there to watch us and cheer us on. Sometimes that meant skipping his lunch at work, or even sneaking away or taking time off to catch a game. He was such a good worker, volunteering when they needed him, that when he needed off, his company worked around it. Nothing was more important than family, and our sports functions or our sisters' cheer or dance functions. Time was tight, and he watched how he spent it very closely, spending every free moment he could with family.

 I hear some parents say, "I don't have a lot of time to spend with my kids, but the time I do is quality time." What is quality time anyway? I would argue that five hours in front of the TV with your kid is worth way more than any one hour of quality time doing just about anything else. You don't know when your son or daughter will need you and open up to you. Quantity trumps quality when it comes to time spent with your loved ones.

That leaves us with effort. Effort is a vigorous or determined attempt at something. Effort can be measured by the energy one spends on something.

 For my dad, effort was everything. When he did something, he did it right. Mowing the lawn, washing a car, or cleaning a furnace, <u>All things worth doing were worth doing right.</u> He put all he could into what he did . . . and that includes raising all of eight of us. He had a lot of help, as my mom was second to none. When we played sports, Dad didn't like it when we lost, but he could always accept it. What he *wouldn't* accept was one of us not giving one hundred percent. He led by example and he expected us to give our all.

And by the way, there is no such thing as giving a hundred and ten percent. Giving more effort than you have, or than even exists, is impossible. Giving a hundred and ten percent is a way of telling someone to give extra effort. But just know if you can give extra effort, you weren't giving a hundred percent to begin with. I know the equation: Effort + Extra Effort $\leq$ 100% Effort.

The energy or effort you possess is limited. No one has an endless supply. Just like your money and your time, you have to figure out where and how to spend your energy. It may be the toughest of the three because it's something you must generate and it isn't easily measured. Money and time are quantifiable. Energy or effort is harder to figure out. Money and time are undeniable when tracked. Effort is more subjective. A great deal of effort to one might be a small amount of effort to another. Some will argue they gave it their all, but others will say they only gave some.

 We spend three things in life: time, money, and effort. In business, it's all about these three precious resources. It helps to have a good plan, but even with a so-so plan, time, money, and effort can lead you to a win. If something isn't working in your business or job, you need only spend more time, money, or effort to improve it. If someone isn't successful at something, it's normally because that person isn't spending enough time, money, or effort on being successful.

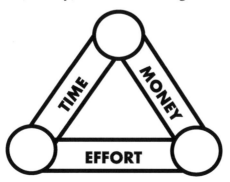

You already now know that if you meet often enough with the right people you can solve any ongoing problem or challenge. The reason is that when you meet often enough you end up spending more time, money, or effort on the problem. It's that simple.

Time, money, and effort are finite. Time is the only thing everyone has an equal amount of. No one gets twenty-five hours in a day.

We each only have so much money (although some might argue that a plastic card can overcome a lack of money . . . at least until the collector shows up).

We only have so much energy or effort to give. Spending more time, money, and effort on recruiting, hiring, retention, advertising, cost savings, delivery systems, safety, you name it, will yield better results.

Consider each one like a bank account. When you invest more time, money, or effort you make a withdrawal on that account. As your balance declines, you have less time, money, or effort to spend on other things. Over time you can generate more money which then can be deposited for other uses, but normally, at least in the short-term, you can only *redistribute* the time, money, and effort you already have. Spend more on any one thing and you then must spend less on something else.

In broad terms, people spend time, money, or effort in the following categories:

- Personal
- Business
- Rest/Relaxation

The typical daily formula for time might be one third (eight hours) for personal, one third for business/work, and one third for sleep, rest, and relaxation. Success sometimes requires different ratios. It's not unusual for the most successful people to spend up to twelve hours a day on business/work, which then leaves less time for personal things and rest and relaxation.

Pulling Back the Curtain

★ Invest your time, money, and effort wisely! Your return will normally be in direct proportion to how much you spend on each. It's a law of physics that for every action there is an equal and opposite reaction. How you spend your time, money, and effort will produce an equal amount of results or outcomes personally, spiritually, and in business.

★ *All things worth doing are worth doing right.* Remember the butterfly effect? Doing things the right way, not the easy way, is a small change that will have a dramatic effect on results and your life.

My Third Trick

The Secret to Success

What is the secret to success? Right decisions. How do you make right decisions? Experience. How do you gain experience? Wrong decisions.
— **Abdul Kalam**

THE SECRET TO SUCCESS? I've wrapped my head around this for years now and have always come back to a very simple way of looking at it.

I first learned it from an audio recording by Earl Nightingale called *The Strangest Secret*. If you haven't listened to this forty-minute audio, I'd highly suggest it. It's very old, but its principles are timeless. Nightingale defines success and then gives you the secret to acquiring it: *You become what you think about.* Think about a worthwhile goal long enough and hard enough . . . and not a bunch of other things at the same time . . . and you can't help but be successful.

What struck me about this simple idea was that it's about *thinking*, not *doing*. If you think about something, long enough and hard enough, you will be successful. Thinking leads to doing, but it's the thinking that's the fuel for the engine that propels you to success. As I look back at my own success, I realize it was driven by thinking about the business—Thinking about it during the day, in the evening,

40

when out with friends, watching TV, and sometimes as I lay my head down to sleep. It consumed me, and others at our business too.

It all starts with the desire to be successful. No desire, means no thinking about it, means no drive to be successful. Desire is the strong wish to do or to have something. It starts in the gut and works its way into everything you do. It produces a restlessness within you and compels you to take steps to be successful.

I'm reminded of something that Joel, a previous HVAC manager, taught me about desire. I'm hardly ever impressed with complicated answers to simple questions, but I'm captivated by simple, easy to understand answers. Joel was one such thinker. In the HVAC business, one of the more difficult challenges is a refrigerant leak. These leaks can occur anywhere along the refrigerant path inside or outside a unit. Your air conditioning system is a closed-loop system, much like your car, so all the refrigerant should be inside a pipe, valve, or coil. There should be no way for it to escape, so when it does you know you have a problem.

There are tools to help locate a leak, but if the leak is small enough the detection equipment will have a difficult time picking it up, especially if it's buried deep within the coil. Many of our techs are good at finding tough-to-spot leaks, others struggle with finding it. Not being technically minded myself, I asked Joel what the trick was to finding small pin-hole refrigerant leaks. Why do some techs find them and others don't even though all have gone through the same training? The answer was an *Aha moment* for me (not to be confused with a *Ta-daaah moment*).

The trick to locating a difficult-to-find refrigerant leak is . . .

⚡ You've got to want to find it badly enough!

That was it. That's all he said. I was expecting some technical answer, some method he used that other techs didn't know about. What he offered was so simple, yet somehow life-changing. It was centered squarely in desire. You've got to want to find it badly enough. Simply profound and profoundly simple!

All technicians want to find it, and most of them do, but when it gets too difficult, some will turn up their desire button. Others don't. I find this to be true for all kinds of personal and business challenges. Some seem to give up much more easily than others, while some are driven to never give up. Some conclude that whatever they're trying to accomplish doesn't work because they couldn't *make* it work. Inject someone else into the same process, with more desire and drive, and ***Ta-daaah*** . . . it works! I see it all the time.

Here's an age-old question that makes a big difference: Can someone's desire be increased significantly enough that they can become more successful? The answer is *yes, no, maybe,* and *sometimes*. I told you I like simple, easy answers, didn't I? The answer to whether someone's desire can be increased is significantly rooted in something else. Now let's back it up one more step: How do we create more desire or drive?

Willingness! You've got to *want* to increase your drive or desire. Desire is the inner drive to succeed. Willingness is the wanting and openness to create that desire. Your willingness involves accepting the fact you need help, it involves learning, and an openness to criticism not just from others but from yourself as well. Willingness is the desire, wish, or readiness to acquire new knowledge, to develop, to improve.

At Parker & Sons, we have Appointment Generators (AGs) in some big-box retail stores whose job is to help customers while informing them of services or products that we provide. Our VP of Retail, Troy, when talking about what makes a successful AG, said, "There are just four things that determine an AG's success: a mind, a mouth, a method, and willingness. All of our AGs have a mind and a mouth. The company has the method. If they are not successful, it's always the fourth ingredient that's missing: willingness." It's that simple.

A lack of willingness is usually rooted in a lack of self-awareness, in not being honest with yourself, or in a lack of acceptance of results or circumstances. Lacking clarity can affect willingness, as well as having low confidence or self-esteem. Willingness leads to desire, which can lead to thinking about success, which translates into doing something, which transforms to accomplishing your goals, which then leads to success.

Our job as leaders and managers is to increase willingness, to learn, to improve, to accept things we cannot change, to change the things we can. Willingness to be open to new ideas, to make room for improvement, to doing *whatever it takes* to hit your goals and that of the company. That's where the magic is.

How can we create or increase willingness?

- Force: Take away all other options. I had heard the phrase *Burn the boats* but I didn't know the history. In 1519, when the conquistador Captain Hernán Cortés landed in Veracruz he reportedly ordered his men to burn the ships in which they had arrived. In essence, he gave them no option but to succeed at the goal of conquest. Survival mode, adrenaline, willingness, and desire kick in quickly when retreat and failure are not options. If taking away all other options can be effective for a conquest, it can certainly be effective for a business, a health issue, a relationship, and many other things.

- Make it public: If you make it known to enough people, especially those who are important to the person in question, likelihood of success increases. No one likes to let their loved ones or those they admire down.
- Persistence: or perseverance, is the hard work you do after you get tired of doing the hard work you already did. Willingness

can increase when someone knows the thing you are working on isn't going away. Be persistent.

- <u>Put money on it</u>: (or some other reward or pain). Personal gain, or loss, can be a powerful motivator, especially to someone who can't afford to lose or doesn't like losing.

- <u>Rewards and accolades</u>: These don't motivate everyone, but when the reward is great enough, willingness can temporarily improve.

- <u>Teach it</u>: The student may or may not learn, but the teacher *always* does. Want someone to get good at something? Have them teach it to someone else.

Ta-daaah!!!!!

Pulling Back the Curtain

★ When hiring for a key position, try to determine the applicant's willingness and desire. Sometimes it can be trying to discover their *Why*. Why do they do what they do? Ask questions around what successes they've had in their life, what they excel in, what they're passionate about, or what they do better than most. Someone who doesn't excel in anything normally lacks the willingness or desire to succeed at anything.

★ As Earl Nightingale said, *You are what you think about.* Think about something long enough and hard enough and you are bound to be successful. Thinking leads to doing. Doing leads to success. What consumes your thoughts?

★ Everybody wants something, but do you want it badly *enough?* If so, you'll normally achieve it. It is always about the *enough.*

Chapter Six

A Snag With the BHAG

Do not let what you cannot do interfere with what you can do.
—**John Wooden**

Jim Collins coined the term *BHAG* in his book *Good to Great*. What is a BHAG? It's a **B**ig **H**airy **A**udacious **G**oal and working toward it became a common corporate mantra. You might not hit it, but even if you miss it, you'll accomplish a lot more than if you had chased a smaller goal. I've often heard, read, and been taught *Reach for the stars and you'll hit the Moon.*

You've heard this philosophy, and if it works for you, great! But it never worked for me. I never saw any sense in setting a goal you don't think you can hit or that's so unreasonable you have to talk yourself into it. Can you really reach the stars? Or even the Moon? I can't. It's too daunting. It requires too much sacrifice. Many people can't relate to it. If something is outside your belief system, you'll surely talk yourself into believing it isn't reasonable.

I'm a small-goal person. Incremental improvement seems reasonable to me. It's easier; it's achievable. If I want to lose weight (and I have many times) I don't set a target of losing fifteen pounds. That's easy to say but hard to do. It's a commitment. It involves life-changing sacrifices. I'd rather set a goal of losing one pound by tomorrow. I can do that. It's not that Big, Hairy, or Audacious. It doesn't involve life-

46

changing sacrifice. And I'll be hitting my goal much sooner: tomorrow! I like hitting goals that I can celebrate with a quick *Ta-daaah*.

Once I hit a small goal it isn't over. That's the difference maker. I reset for a new goal, maybe another pound by the next day, another pound the day after that, and eventually maybe another pound every two days. Hitting smaller short-term goals leads to more success. I'm two weeks into the diet and I've lost eight or nine pounds. *Now* I'm motivated. Now I may end up losing fifteen pounds, and maybe I had that number in my head as the ultimate BHAG, but psychologically I find that small goals are way more important. I don't focus on reaching for the stars to hit the Moon. I concentrate on reaching for the next rung on the ladder. I do that every day, every month, every year, and then look back down the ladder to . . . Oh my gosh! I'm way up here, closer to the stars than ever.

I use diets as an example because it's one of the most common goals people have, and unfortunately, one of the most unsuccessful aspirations. I'm six feet tall and fluctuate between a hundred and ninety and two hundred pounds. When I get to two hundred (or maybe two hundred and two ☺) I get disgusted and start working my way back down to a hundred and ninety. It may not be my ideal weight according to the chart at the doctor's office, but a weight I can talk myself into is ideal for me. I even invented a diet, the PK Rotational (PK stands for my initials, but I never tell people that). Some tell me they've heard of it, which is funny because it's never been published and only my family and friends know about it.

I like the simplicity of the diet and how it gives you something to look forward to the next day. <u>It's a short-term diet to lose a little weight quickly; it's not a lifestyle change</u>. It's pretty simple (See the appendix if you'd like to know more. I guess it's published after all!).

Losing weight, or getting in shape, is a discipline. It involves willpower and sacrifice, no matter what plan you're on. Success in business or your job is similar. It too involves certain disciplines to achieve success.

And if people like achieving goals they'll like *beating them* even more. The more you beat a goal, the more rewarding and motivated you become. If I lose two pounds in a day, and my goal was to lose one pound, I'm elated. It motivates me for the next goal.

Beating goals can be addictive and habit-forming. falling short of goals is the same. Measuring results against your goals is important too. The more closely you can measure results, and the more closely you can measure them against a time frame (e.g., daily or even real time), the more apt you are to effect changes which would lead to hitting your goals. Not really knowing how you are doing until the end of the month is not a recipe for success.

At Parker & Sons we have a reasonable monthly goal, and we measure daily and month-to-date how we're doing against that goal. The department managers and dispatch, via our software, look at how we're doing throughout each day. Something magical happens when you know your short-term goal and measure how you're doing. And if you layer on rewards for hitting and beating goals, you reinforce the willingness and drive and, more importantly, demonstrate that you are willing to share the company's success with those who do the hard work of achieving and beating their goals.

 When you create reasonable goals and develop a culture of beating the tar out of them, you develop a culture of winning. And nothing could be more important within a company than developing a culture of winning. People like to be winners and part of a team that wins. Success breeds success. I don't believe in the saying *Winning isn't everything, it's the only thing*, in the philosophy of winning at all costs. I also don't believe in the phrase *It's not whether you win or lose, it's how you play the game.* I believe in both. It *is* how you play the game. And it's not *all* about winning. But if you're going to play the game, let's set a goal of winning it.

Sometimes you might need to redefine *winning*. It might not be about short-term revenue increases. It might not be about short-term profit. In the long term, for a business, it had better be about *both*. In a tough month, winning might be defined as breaking even. It could be defined as not having an any accidents. It could be about hitting a customer satisfaction rating, reducing turnover, or hitting a staffing goal. Setting out to do something, and everyone working together to get there, and achieving that something, is winning. And winning is a powerful feeling.

People ask me all the time, "Wow, you went from seven million to over two hundred million. You must have had some master plan, some BHAGs, some blueprint and awesome vision you created to get there." I always answer the same way: "No. No BHAGs, no big goals, no master plan, no blueprint, no vision, and certainly no magic sauce. Just a bunch of good people doing extraordinary things and getting marginally better at something every day, every month, every year. When I bought the company, I just wanted to make payroll and be able to pay the bills. That was the master plan. But when we did eight million I *wanted* to do nine million. When we did nine million I *wanted* to do eleven million. Things snowballed and we gained momentum. Now our goals are bigger, but still very attainable."

🚩 Pulling Back the Curtain

★   Any big goal can be broken up into smaller goals and benchmarks. People love hit-ting goals and especially *beating* goals. To create a *winning* culture, at work or at home with your children, create smaller goals and celebrate beating them. Then reset on another small goal on your way to the BHAG.

★   What is measured gets improved. We've all heard variations of this famous business lesson. Why does that happen? When you keep score you know how you're doing. And when you know how you're doing, especially when comparing to a goal, you naturally want to do better.

★   Measure what's important. Measuring activity, attempts, failures, and effort can be just as important as measuring end results.

My Fourth Trick

Grow Like a Fish

A shark in a fish tank will grow eight inches, but in the ocean it will grow to eight feet or more. The shark will never outgrow its environment and the same is true about you. Many times we're around small thinking people so we don't grow. Change your environment and watch your growth.
—Bob Harrison

WHEN TRISHA AND I GOT MARRIED, and maybe for fifteen years after, we had fish. Watching fish was relaxing and taking care of them was enjoyable. I experimented with different kinds of fish, different sizes of tanks and filtration systems, and got pretty good at keeping the fish alive and healthy. We had Oscars and got into feeding them the live fish and watching nature take its course, and Betta fish, who are very aggressive, especially with other Betta fish. They loved to go tank jumping, like jumping out of the tank and onto the floor. We had a pet lizard who used to like to escape the tank as well (his version of an escape room), and then we'd have to go on a lizard hunt throughout the basement. We also had crabs who liked to catch fish in their pincers. Once we even saw them catch a pregnant fish as she delivered her babies. The crab had the mother in its claw and was eating the babies as they came out. It was simultaneously fascinating and disturbing. The kids watched in disbelief while my wife sprang into action and grabbed a wooden spoon, hitting the crab until he let go of the mother fish. Being a nurse, Trisha was familiar with the wooden spoon technique to save lives. She saved about five baby fish and we spent the next few months watching them grow.

> One of the things I learned was that fish grow in proportion to the size of their tank and the number of other fish that are in it. The larger the tank, the larger the fish. The fewer the tankmates, the larger the fish. A small tank filled with fish will curtail growth dramatically. It dawned on me: Companies and people are just like fish.

Over the course of my career in the home-services business I've seen and visited maybe a hundred companies. And in that time, with very few exceptions (I could count them on one hand), the size of the business tended to emulate the size of the building. Small one, two, or three-truck operations were either operating out of their home or were in a thousand-square-foot office. two-to-three-million-dollar companies were in three-to-four-thousand-square-foot buildings. Medium-sized companies, doing six to twelve million dollars, were in six-to-eight-thousand-square-foot buildings. If I saw their sales flatten out at some level, invariably they had maxed out in their building as well. They had run out of room to grow. Sometimes it wasn't the size of the building as much as it might be the size of their lot. Parking, or room to operate or store equipment, can limit a company as well.

Buy a bigger building, add more parking or yard to operate in, expand your footprint to another area of town, buy more vans and trucks, hire more technicians, and almost without exception a company will start to grow again. I've often been asked, "If there's one thing you could tell a fellow business owner that would help them grow their business, what would it be?"

I answer the same way every time: "Hire more techs."

"But what if I can't keep them busy?"

I always answer, "But what if you *can?* Assuming you are at or near capacity with your current techs, you can't grow the business without growing the techs doing the work and generating revenue." As it's said in *Field of Dreams*, "If you build it, they will come." *Like fish, you will grow to the size of the tank you are in.*

Growing the size of your tank is not always a physical thing, like a building, a parking lot, a yard, vehicles, a satellite facility, or employees. Growing the size of your tank can also be mental: capabilities, drive, leadership, and talent. Expanding your mind is probably one of the most powerful tank expansions you can invest in. By reading or listening to this book, if I did my job right, you'll expand your tank of skills, which will lead to you improving yourself personally or professionally. Seminars, mentors, books, videos, peer groups, training, coaches, self-reflection and assessment, competitors, visiting successful companies, are all ways to expand your skill tank. If I'm any good as a leader, it's because of all the influencers I've had in my life. Investing in the personal growth of your leaders, managers, supervisors, and soon-to-be supervisors is imperative for them to expand their tank of skills to continue growing. Expanding the size of your leadership's tank is not only a great return on investment, it's a requirement if you want your business to continue to grow.

Expanding your tank can also be a matter of self-image or self-belief. How many times have you heard someone say that they aren't good enough or smart enough, that they can't play at a high enough level to compete, that they don't have what it takes to be better than they are? One way to guarantee that all of the above is true is to tell yourself that and believe it. Convincing yourself that you are less than your potential is like shrinking your own tank. Instead, tell yourself that not only are you good enough, you're *better* than good enough. A positive self-image, and actively telling yourself that you have what it takes to succeed, is like moving into a bigger tank.

Expanding your tank isn't just a concept for businesses; it can be for personal growth as well. Want to get that next promotion or make more money? Expand your tank of skills, of accomplishments, of volunteering, of thinking differently, of ideas, of improvements. Want to be a better husband? Expand your tank of looking at what you love about your wife, not about what you don't. Want to be a better parent? Expand the tank of time and energy you spend with your children. Expand your tank of skills by reading about parenthood or spending time with other great parents. Or buy a fish tank for your kid, take care of it together, and watch this concept revealed firsthand.

We covered how the size of the tank affects the size of the fish, but what about how the number of fish in the tank? Remember when I mentioned my first entry into the home services arena when I landed a job with Roto-Rooter? That company had a long history of growth and success, becoming the number-one brand in the drain-cleaning space. They did incredibly well by driving a brand that screams drain cleaning. However, they struggled with bolting on plumbing as an additional service. You would think that plumbing and drain cleaning go together, but not for Roto-Rooter. It took them years to overcome being a drain-cleaning-only company, to being a plumbing company.

Roto-Rooter locations that had long histories of growth were flattening out. Some hadn't grown sales in three or four years. These were in big markets and the trend seemed to be expanding. It was just one or two cities in the beginning; now it had grown to five or six. Spencer Lee, one of the smartest and most competitive leaders I know, and now the CEO of Roto-Rooter, came up with a theory much like the fish-tank story. It was simple, just how I like it. He called it *Optisizing*.

Optisizing—There is an optimum revenue size for every location. That size will be influenced by the market you are in, by competition, by the economy, by the labor pool, licensing or regulatory constraints, weather patterns, by many factors . . . but none of the factors, even collectively, will be as great as one major factor . . . YOU!

YOU . . . meaning the person running the location. YOU have an optimum size of location or department you can run. And YOU can reach your capacity to grow the location, department, or sales. The location can outgrow your capabilities, your desire, your skill set, your ability to handle the challenges. YOU are the limiting factor. When sales flatten, YOU'VE probably reached your location's optimum size, based on YOU.

The solution? Split the location into two smaller locations, normally geographically, so that you resize what YOU are responsible for.

So Spencer tried it in Hartford, in Boston, in New York, and then in Philly. Eventually they tried it in Chicago. The eight-million-dollar location was split into an east and west location, each doing approximately four million. The leader of the larger location now had a much smaller location, and they had to hire another leader for the other location. Each of the two locations started growing again and, if memory serves me right, each grew a million dollars a year for the next two years. It was now a twelve-million-dollar market, the west doing six and a half and the east doing five and a half. Revenue flattened out again at that point, so they opened north and south locations, optisizing yet again, each of the four locations starting with around three to four million each. And without fail, they started growing again. Roto-Rooter duplicated this across the company. Optisizing was a huge success.

> What was at play here was that each leader had reached his or her optimum size, based on their capabilities, skills, desires, and capacity. Their tank was too full of trucks, of employees, of daily problems and challenges, of customer issues, of turnover, of corporate initiatives, and daily fires that needed to be put out. There is no room to grow in a full tank. And unfortunately, Roto-Rooter didn't invest or have systems in place to quickly expand the skill tanks of their leadership. The answer was to take some of the problems and daily challenges out of the tank and put them in another tank. *Optisizing!* It was brilliant! Now long term, I would argue that investing in training that expands a leader's capabilities is a better formula, but it is an investment in time, money, and energy that most companies simply don't make.

Roto-Rooter had a saying to describe a location that was doing poorly: *It's not the land, it's the man.* Now that obviously would go for women too, they just wanted it to rhyme ☺. When a location was doing poorly, and you asked that leader why, they always responded with reasons outside of their control. It was outside forces acting upon them that caused the poor results. It was the market, the economy, consumers who weren't spending, unemployment, competition, weather, industry trends, political temperature, and the list goes on and on. After I left Roto-Rooter, I even heard one division manager blaming the events and aftermath of 9/11 . . . which might have made sense in 2001 or a year or two after, but this was *ten years later.* "We just never really recovered after 9/11." Really?

It's not the land, it's the man was our gut check with everyone that the problem isn't any of those outside forces, and your city or market (or land) is not materially different from others. It's *you*, my friend. Harsh realities are sometimes sobering. But it was a saying that caught on quickly and everyone knew that using outside forces as the reason for doing poorly, over a long-time frame (e.g. two to three years), simply wasn't going to fly. You better take responsibility for yourself.

Taking fish out of the tank to make more room for growth can also mean terminating employees who either covertly or overtly tear your company down. It's hard to grow a company when you have a small handful doing what they can to make sure you *can't* grow. Listen to them, consider their complaints, fix what is broken, but constant and consistent bad influencers are better off working for a competitor. Removing obstacles is another form of taking fish out of the tank. Improving operating systems, delivery systems, reducing turnover, and a whole host of other obstacles, are all ways to reduce the number of fish slowing down your organization.

Another strategy that some companies, consolidators, and investors employ is removing some of the fish in their market tank by purchasing competitors: Consolidate three smaller fish into one bigger fish. This strategy can work by giving the combined fish the buying power, marketing clout, operational efficiencies, or leadership that it needs to dominate a market. It can work if executed well. Be cautious though: I've seen business plans that are convincing on paper, showing that $1+1+1 = 5$ only to find out that, when implemented, 1+1+1 = 1.5 or, even worse, less than 1. Buying your way to market share can be a dangerous strategy. Organic growth, not growth through acquisition, is always the best measure of the real success of a business. Grow your own company first. Once you are good at organic growth, then strategic acquisitions can make a lot of sense.

Want more growth in your company or for yourself? Use this trick: Expand your tank or take some fish out of it. It's not the only way to grow, but it's one of the best ones.

Ta-daaah!!!!!!!!

Pulling Back the Curtain

★   People and businesses, like fish, grow to the size of the tank they are in and how many other fish are in it with them. Build a big tank of capabilities. Expand your tank of skills continuously. And clear your tank of distractions, nay-sayers, and non-productive activity that compete for your time, energy, and focus.

★   YOU are why you will be successful. And YOU are why you won't be. Nothing can stop YOU from success, but there is someone who can. That someone is YOU. *Whether you think you can, or you think you can't—you're right.*—Henry Ford

★   No good fish (you) goes anywhere (in life) without a porpoise. *Ha ha ha ha ha!* Had to end my fish analogy with a dad joke 😊.

Chapter Seven

Making More Out of the Business You Already Get

Chase money, and money will run from you, and you will become its slave. Chase a purpose, and money will run to you, and it will become your slave.
—**Rick Hutcherson**

WHEN VINCE AND I BOUGHT THE COMPANIES IN PHOENIX FROM BLUE DOT, we had to decide what to concentrate on to build a foundation for growth. We weren't making much money, so our funds were limited. I started to formulate our plan and shared it with Vince, my partner. Vince "noodled" on it (That's what he called it). He also liked to say, "I've got a pocket full of pennies, so let me give you my two-cents worth." He and I worked together well and enjoyed bouncing ideas off of each other. With few other options, it seemed to make sense to grow our business from within first. Why spend time, money, and energy on bringing in *new* business when we already had a lot of existing customers who might want to do *more* business with us?

 Our plan: Let's make more out of the business we already have

To do that we had to make sure we were providing exceptional service and *WOWing* our customers. With just some minor tweaks we started delivering more value than ever before. After that was accomplished, we began to focus on turning one call into two, increasing our average two-hundred-dollar service ticket to three or four hundred dollars. We improved our HVAC system leads from our service base, and we improved our close rate on HVAC system sales from thirty to thirty-five percent, and eventually as high as fifty percent. We improved our ninety-percent customer satisfaction rating to over ninety-five percent. We turned our regular customers into *loyal* customers through our maintenance agreements, which we later called the Parker Family Plan. And we wowed our customers so much they couldn't help but share their experiences with others, resulting in an endless stream of referrals. All of these initiatives were things I was good at because they were the very things I had concentrated on for years when I traveled to other locations or companies to help them grow their businesses.

Over the next two years, with a lot of persistence and perseverance, we got crazy good at making more business out of the business we already had. Isn't that where any business should start? Why try to drive new business in the door when your low-hanging fruit is already in the room? We dissected each customer interaction and started perfecting our plan and its *execution.* In the next couple of chapters I'll tell you how we did it.

Chapter Eight

The Incoming Call or Click

People don't care how much you know until they know how much you care.
—**Theodore Roosevelt**

IT ALL STARTS WITH A PHONE CALL OR A CLICK. Back in 2004 it was always a phone call, but the process hasn't changed. From the moment the phone rings, there are so many hurdles to get over. In my travels of helping companies grow, I can tell you that many contractors lose as many calls as they capture. Even the best companies seemed to lose a significant number of calls, over ten percent. Those that weren't up there with the best were losing as much as fifty percent.

The problem with losing calls is that you *don't know what you're losing.* The call you didn't answer or couldn't close, could be a vendor, a wrong number, a customer kicking tires, a seventy-nine-dollar tune-up, a five-hundred-dollar repair, or a thirty thousand-dollar HVAC three-system sale. Who knows which one it is? When you decide not to answer a call (and it really is a *decision* when you know you aren't answering them all) you're deciding to pass on that thirty-thousand-dollar sale. Who, if they knew it was a thirty-thousand-dollar sale, would decide not to answer the call? No one would! And yet, whether on purpose or by accident, that decision is made every day in virtually every organization.

A few years ago, I asked our team how many customer calls they think we lose each day. I heard ten, twenty, thirty on average. That may sound like a lot, because it is, but on a real hot day in Phoenix we can take over *four thousand calls*. As a percentage, we're losing one to two percent, so what's the big deal? You're about to find out.

Now, if those are the numbers they were *admitting* to losing, I figured it was probably higher than that. We used thirty as our example. Our service calls averaged four hundred dollars, but HVAC installations averaged nine thousand dollars. Water heater installations were fourteen hundred dollars. Blended, all calls in the mix, the average call generated seven hundred and fifty dollars. We estimated we were losing thirty calls a day. $750 x 30 calls a day x 260 working days, not even counting weekend work, = $5,850,000 in lost revenue each year *because we weren't answering the phone well*. Wow! Now over a ten-year period, that's almost sixty million dollars in revenue. And that's not even considering lost referrals, which could be that much again. Could we possibly be okay with losing that much business by not being good at answering every call?

With this in mind, back in 2004, we had to come up with a strategy, or a new way of thinking, about incoming phone calls. The answer seemed simple . . .

We need to answer all the calls all the time. We must have a battle cry: **Don't Lose One Call**.

Given our business was seasonal (both HVAC and plumbing), and given that call volume for HVAC was really weather driven, we needed a way to handle spikes in call volume during a month, within a week, and throughout the day. Without getting too deeply into the weeds with all the answers, we basically decided that the most important part of anyone's job, which meant *everyone's* job, was to answer the phone. And during peaks in call volume we would enlist the help of accounting, of HR, supervisors, managers, and even myself. Our outbound call center was converted to an inbound call center when the need arose. And so, the calls we used to lose we started to answer.

Now answering the phone is just step one, and we got exceptionally good at it. Closing or booking the call is step two, and it's the more important step. Booking the call requires answering three questions:

- Can we meet the needs or solve the problem?
- Can we do it within the requested time frame?
- If raised by the customer, can we do it at an acceptable price?

Can we meet the needs or solve the problem? This was the easiest step. Back then, we did heating, AC, plumbing, and drain cleaning. If the request was within these trades we could probably help them. We didn't do large commercial work or new construction, but any break/fix or new installation was within our capability. Later we added water softening/RO, electrical, and insulation to our arsenal.

Can we do it within the requested time frame? This was a bit more challenging. Our goal was, and still is, to provide same-day service for any emergency, same-day/next-day service for all other services, and convenient times to book any service several days out should the customer want to wait. Much of our business is "emergency" related. When your AC goes out in Phoenix in July it's an emergency. When water is coming through your ceiling it's an emergency. When you run out of hot water, or can't use your toilets, or your electricity goes out . . . You get the idea. These are not things people want to wait days to fix, so response time was paramount.

It then became the age-old economics equation of supply and demand. When your call demand exceeds your supply of technicians you have a dilemma. Most businesses have this problem. I see it with home-service companies, but I also see it in restaurants, bars, fast-food drive-throughs, checkout lines at stores, entertainment, airlines, and so many others. What can you do when too many want your product or service, at the same time or in close proximity, and you can't serve them all timely enough?

It's called *triage* and hospitals are masters at it. They prepare for it, they practice it, and they execute it. Now, it might not always be pretty. Situations can change minute to minute and there are things that don't get thought out perfectly, but somehow, some way, hospitals do what is needed and save so many lives. As I write this chapter, the COVID-19 pandemic is in full swing with over seven hundred thousand deaths in the U.S. alone. I've read so many stories of hospitals running out of masks and other PPE, of shortages of ventilators, beds, rooms, oxygen, of places to care for and preserve those who have passed on. Yet somehow, some way, they make do, they improvise and give exceptional care, saving thousands of lives. My hat is off to all those who care for those who are sick or dying, and the sacrifice they make, personally and professionally, on everyone's behalf. It's truly remarkable.

If hospitals and other medical facilities can triage effectively, *so can we*. We started prioritizing calls for those who had health conditions and needed to be in air conditioning, for hospitals and medical facilities who were without AC and needed help, for homes which were being destroyed by water damage from floods due to plumbing issues. We sent our supervisors out to run calls. We send those finishing up training on calls and had the managers walk them through how to fix the problems. We cross trained some techs into other trades to help. We worked long and we worked hard. We still do. It's truly remarkable what our plumbers, electricians, AC techs, water techs, and all our installers, and all those who support them, especially dispatch, do during high-peak days. And when the day is over, they know the next day, just like a hospital during triage, will likely bring much of the same. It's why, if I see any technicians, plumbers, electricians, or installers in our industry, at a gas station, a restaurant, or out and about, I introduce myself and thank them for being in our industry. They are truly remarkable people who care about taking care of others.

Now we don't get to everyone during extreme spikes, but we do get to most, and normally within that same-day/next-day time frame. We hire some extra technicians to handle peaks, and when the spikes don't hit, we have to fight to keep them busy and productive. Overall, I think we do a better job than any competitor in our market in providing timely service. Which brings us to . . .

If raised by the customer, can we do it at an acceptable price? When it is truly an emergency, price often doesn't come up. They just want us out there as quickly as possible, and what they spend is a little farther down the list. But price is eventually a factor, and ultimately, if someone uses you repeatedly, they must feel good about the price/value relationship you provide.

Most people don't mind spending a little extra for above-average service. I learned from Bill Griffin, then CEO of Roto-Rooter, "You'll never get mad at yourself for hiring or owning the best. You'll kick yourself in the butt, though, for trying to save a little money and finding out that the thing you bought or the company you hired wasn't capable of providing what you really wanted or needed. And then you wasted all your money. Always hire or buy the best. Even when they screw up, and occasionally everyone does, they'll fix it . . . and then some."

 It made sense back then and it makes even more sense now. I heard the same from many trainers in our industry over the years. I learned a long time ago, *"I'd rather explain our pricing to customers once than apologize for poor service forever."*

So we train our customer service representatives (CSRs) to build value and explain all the things we do that other companies don't . . . all the steps we take, the training we provide, the inventory we carry, the industry-leading guarantees we offer, and how quickly we handle their emergency. All that said, price can still be something that customers shop for, so we decided to do five things . . .

- We wouldn't charge extra for nights, weekends, or holidays (most of our competition does). AC, plumbing, and electrical are more likely to break when you use them the most: at night, and on weekends and holidays when family is over. We didn't want customers paying extra because of that.
- We weren't going to charge a "trip charge" just to show up. Some companies do charge just to come out. Just showing up doesn't work in sports, in business, or in life. You should *do* something to *charge* something.

- We would charge a small seventy-nine-dollar diagnostic fee that would cover our tech finding out what the problem is (which can take anywhere from a few minutes to an hour or more), finding a solution (sometimes easy, sometimes not), and providing a repair/replace estimate. **If the customer wanted us to do the work, we'd waive that seventy-nine-dollar fee.**

- And we'd compare our pricing with other leading companies in Phoenix, overlay with what some of the best companies in America were charging, and *be in the middle of that mix*, not comparing ourselves with the "Johnny Lunch Bucket" companies, but with the *best* companies. We hired a service to help us with that, and they produced our price book.

- We'd give free estimates for any new equipment installations like heating/AC equipment, water heaters, water softeners/RO, electrical panels, etc. We didn't want people feeling pressured for bigger-ticket items.

All of these factors helped us—and still help us—tell the story that we care about what we charge people, we want to make sure our customers get exceptional value, we won't gouge people when they call us at odd hours, and we want to protect customers from overpaying. This doesn't mean that there aren't competitors who charge less than we do. There are hundreds, many of whom aren't licensed, don't carry insurance, won't stand behind their work, are without guarantees, don't background-check their employees, don't show up when they say they will, trash your home, and many other meaningful differences. And there are some competitors that charge more than we do, too.

So, we've answered the call, we've booked the call, we're getting ready to thank the customer and hang up . . . but there's one more thing to accomplish. We call it *Opportunity Calls*. While you have them on the phone, tell them about something else we do or offer. It's the equivalent of ordering a hamburger and the attendant asking *Would you like fries with that?* Or on Amazon, *People who bought X also bought Y.* Ending the call is an opportunity to tell the customer something else we offer or to ask if there's anything else we could help them with.

If someone called for plumbing, they would soon learn that we also do heating and AC, and we'd highlight a special we had going on at the time. They might be interested, they might not be. We don't try to talk them into anything, we simply make sure they know we have other services and that they know about our specials, maybe not for now, maybe not for tomorrow, but down the road for sure. The incoming call, which we answered quickly and booked, could now be worth two calls, sometimes even three. It's amazing what a simple "Got any slow running drains, leaky faucets, or toilet problems?" at the end of a call can do.

 The CSR gets a spiff from booking the extra business, so they make extra money as well. Some of them make as much or more in spiffs as they do with their hourly pay. We have CSRs who make the equivalent of forty dollars an hour. In addition to add-on services the CSRs can also recommend membership in the Parker Family Plan maintenance program. Maintenance agreements build fences around your customers and keep the competition out. They can also smooth out lulls in business during slower months or seasons.

In summary, we got pretty good at answering the phone, closing/booking calls, and ending each call with another opportunity. These seem like simple concepts, and they are, but some companies aren't good at them, just like some football teams aren't good at blocking and tackling. Getting good at the fundamentals is always the best place to start. We paid to make the phone ring, we might as well be good at answering it.

Is your company crazy good at being responsive when someone reaches out to you or are you losing business? To expand the concept: Are you responsive to the needs of your employees or are you too busy to help them? Are you responsive personally when your kid craves your attention, or when your spouse or loved one needs you to listen while they vent? Examine how responsive you or your company is when someone needs you. This isn't even low-hanging fruit. It's fruit that has already fallen. You only need to pick it up.

📷 Pulling Back the Curtain

★   Some companies spend a lot of money to get the phone to ring (or generate an online lead), and then don't answer it when it does . . . or they aren't good at interacting with the customer. Concentrate on what you have before you before you search for what lies ahead. *"Your diamonds are not in far distant mountains or in yonder seas; they are in your own backyard, if you but dig for them"* — Russell H. Conwell.

★   Figure out what your customers value the most then give it to them. Today's consumer wants high-quality service and products at a fair price (I didn't say *low* price), and they want it when they want it. In our business, that usually means NOW.

★   What is your "would you like fries with that"? Sometimes, consumers don't know how much they want something until they're asked.

Chapter Nine

The Service Call

Customer service shouldn't be a department. It should be the entire company.
—**Tony Hsieh**

NOW WE'VE BOOKED THE CALL, maybe added on an opportunity, and we're ready to run the call. This is the make-or-break moment and it's driven by who gets sent to your house. There's so much anxiety around some stranger showing up and entering your home. What will they look like? What kind of value system do they have? Are they honest or are they going to make up repairs and charge an exorbitant amount of money? Will they clean up after themselves or trash my house? Will they respect me and my family . . . and my belongings? Will they be able to fix it? Will it stay fixed? Do they have a criminal record? Are they having a good day and will I pay for it if they're not? We know there's anxiety and sometimes fear when strangers come to your home. I'm in the business and I have a level of it myself when someone I don't know comes over.

 Who we send into a home will ultimately determine if we win or lose. What customers want, in a word, is TRUST. Can I trust this person to do the right thing, to take care of my things, to not make up repairs, to fix the problem, and to charge me appropriately? And can I trust the company to stand behind it and make it right if I'm unhappy? <u>TRUST is what the customer is really buying</u>. So trust is what we want to make sure we have in spades, not just in the customer's mind, but in reality as well. **We need to be the most trusted provider in Phoenix and not just say we are, like so many other companies do. We need to be able to prove it!**

So we developed a trust certification process, a way of knowing we had trustworthy employees, and share it with the customers. We'll concentrate on our technicians and installers for this chapter, but all employees go through a process. All technicians are *Trust Certified*® through a stringent ten-step process.

1. Background check
2. Drug screening
3. Driving record
4. Interview with supervisor
5. Interview with department head
6. Interview with HR (an all-female team which gives us a female perspective in a male-dominated field)
7. Licensed (where required), bonded, and insured
8. Shows up in well-marked van
9. Shows up in uniform
10. Trained in customer skills and the Parker experience

Much of our competition doesn't clear these hurdles. Beyond this ten-step process, during the interview process, and with the homework we do, we're trying to find something very simple: Is this a nice person and can we, and our customers, trust him or her? That's it: a nice, trustworthy person. It's important they have some technical skills, depending on the position, but we can *teach* technical skills. We can't easily teach someone to be nice or trustworthy, and niceness is largely a matter of making an impression. Is this a person that we would have over to our own house for dinner? Hang around? Laugh and have fun with? And trust with our own kids, our own house, our own money? If so, and if they pass our ten-step process, they are Trust Certified.

Does this mean we never get it wrong? No. We do get it wrong sometimes, but not often. You don't *really* know who you're hiring until they get on the job. When we make a bad hire we normally catch it within ninety days and then we cut our losses. We weed out those who don't fit in. Being nice and trustworthy is not an option at our company. It's mandatory. It's who we are!

Just like you must have the right ingredients for a recipe to taste good, you also have to have the right employees for the service experience to feel good. No company can charge so little that trust becomes unimportant, although many try. And no company can overcome a culture of being untrustworthy without tearing down the organization from top to bottom.

We recruit, hire, and retain TRUST in the team members we have. We knew we had the best team members of any company, but we needed to make sure. And we needed someone else to attest to it if we were going to claim it. We had gotten feedback and awards from the manufacturers we used, from our vendors, from our advertisers, from non-profits we had helped, from organizations we supported. And we had hundreds, and eventually thousands, of customer-satisfaction letters, emails, and calls. What we needed, though, was independent verification.

That came in a big way in 2006 when we won the Better Business Bureau's Torch Award for Business Ethics. Ethics sounds a lot like trust to me. We were, according to the BBB, the most ethical business in Phoenix in our size classification. We not only won against our contractor competitors, but all *other* companies too. WOW! Now that's meaningful. And the BBB is an independent body who had no ties to us . . . and trust me, they did plenty of homework to reach their conclusion. We were nominated other years as well, were a finalist, and won again in 2014. Repeat winners are always a rarity, but no other company has repeated this feat in the home services industry, an industry that is not always the most trusted.

We were also recognized in 2014 with a Certificate of Special Congressional Recognition, honored by the United States House of Representatives and David Schweikert, Arizona's Sixth Congressional District Representative.

In 2008, we were voted number one by consumers in *Ranking Arizona*, Arizona's premier opinion poll of companies in the Valley. WOW!!!! Another independent ranking voted upon by consumers. What could be better? I'll tell you what could: We won it in 2008 and every year since, for a record-breaking fourteen-year streak in our category. Consumers were telling us they loved us and trusted us. This seemed to mirror what we are seeing online, with our seven thousand-plus reviews on Google and 4.7-star rating, our near five-star BBB rating, our Facebook 4.7 rating, our Angie's List Super Service Award, Pearl Certification award, and many other awards and ratings.

We've won many other awards throughout the years, many of them very prestigious. Winning awards, especially those that radiate ethics or trust, verify to us that we continue to do the right thing, which means the techs we send into homes, besides passing our Trust Certification process and being

73

nice, are also award winning, as are the rest of our team members.

We came a long way in this chapter just to establish trust as the main ingredient on every service call, but I wanted to firmly implant just how important it is. Most books talk about customer-service skills, communication, selling techniques, or how to develop the perfect service call, including where to park, how to walk to the front door, why to knock first versus ringing the doorbell, putting on shoe covers, etc. We do all of those things, but it all pales in comparison to having trustworthy techs and the homeowner knowing it. Once trust is established, everything else is easy.

1. Listen to the customer
2. Ask questions
3. Make a thorough diagnosis (prescription without a thorough diagnosis is malpractice)
4. Develop solutions
5. Give options with pricing
6. Educate the customer about the options
7. Let the customer decide what is best for them
8. Get approval before starting any work
9. Complete the work and be thorough in everything you do
10. Go over your work with the customer
11. Answer any questions/concerns
12. Have customer sign, indicating their satisfaction

There are techniques for doing all of the above, but in the interest of this chapter taking too many trees (for those who bought the paper book), we'll punt that to another time or another forum.

Trust is an all-important attribute that you want others to have in you or your business. Trust can be given up front. You've heard the

phrase *I trust you until I don't.* That's someone who trusts everyone until they're given a reason not to. For others, trust is rarely
given; it must be earned. Their philosophy is *I trust no one until
they've earned it.* Whether given or earned, once trust is broken,
it's sometimes impossible to get back. It can take months or years,
and sometimes can't be mended at all.

But there's good news for companies: Consumers in general are
fairly forgiving if you recognize and admit the shortcoming, apologize, and work to repair the damage. Some of them can become your
biggest fans. I've found that most people are also forgiving in their
personal affairs, depending on how deep the cut is or how many
times one is burnt.

Customers normally don't get to see or hear me or the other managers and supervisors at our company. They hear the customer service representative and they experience the technician or installer.
When one of our technicians makes a home visit, that person *is* Parker & Sons to the customer, just like a teacher is everything to the
student and parents. Bad teachers in a good school can ruin a student
or their ability to learn. Good teachers in a less desirable school can
propel a student to exceptional learning, better grades, and more op-
portunities. Make sure you surround yourself and your company
with the best people, and that you and others establish trust in all
you do. It pays big dividends in life and in business.

Pulling Back the Curtain

★ Since the technician or installer is ultimately Parker & Sons to the customer, it's vitally important he or she is someone who your customer will love. Is this someone the customer would enjoy having over for dinner? We can teach the technical skills, but the soft skills are sometimes much harder to ingrain.

★ In golf, it is said *drive for show, putt for dough*, meaning putting is where the game is won or lost. Who you send into someone's home, serves you in a restaurant, or takes care of you in the hospital is where the game is won or lost.

★ Trust is what people are wanting and buying in any service and in many products. Trust is what you need to be selling. Saying you are "the most trusted company" doesn't make you the most trusted. Winning awards that radiate trust will.

Chapter Ten

Games People Play

Successful people do what unsuccessful people are unwilling to do. Don't wish it were easier; wish you were better.
—**Jim Rohn**

THERE IS A GAME THAT EVERYONE PLAYS. The two opponents are fierce competitors. Each one wants to dominate you and each one controls your ultimate success in life, in business, in relationships, as a parent, as a friend, as a pet owner, your relationship with God, everything. This game we all play is called . . .

How little can I do? vs. How much can I do?

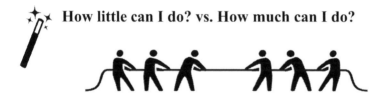

You're playing the game right now. Some, hopefully most, are playing the game on the *How much can I do* side. How much can I do to read this book, concentrate, reflect, make notes, maybe even set goals, and get as much out of this book as possible. Others are playing on the *How little can I do?* side. They'll still read the book, get something out of it, but maybe be distracted, doing other things at the same time, skipping some chapters, only reading the "wanded" sections, trying to find the meat, and willing to sacrifice content to save time.

This game goes on all day, with virtually everything we do. When I grew up, sports were important to me, school not so much. I played the *How much can I do?* game with sports and the *How little can I do?* game with school. How little can I do and still get an A? Doing the homework if I had to turn it in, but not doing it if I didn't. Waiting until the last day to start a project or study for a test, cramming all night. What happens? I was smart enough to get lots of A's, but often got B's and occasionally a C. No scholarship for this guy. But if I had a basketball game that afternoon and we'd just got a foot of snow I'd be shoveling the driveway to make sure I was tuned up come game time.

Our son Josh and our daughter Justine played a different game in school. Josh could turn it on and off and went in and out of the game for school, sometimes playing *How much can I do?,* and at other times, if his average was high enough, he'd toy with *How little can I do?* thinking he had his A secured. He balanced sports, working out, and fun. He got virtually all A's, with an occasional B sprinkled in. Josh was a smart cookie and school seemed like it was easier for him, but make no mistake, it took a lot of hard work to earn his grades. He got a scholarship to college because of his grades, covering much of his tuition. He now plays the *How much can I do?* game with his very successful business, his marriage, and now as a father too. Certainly, a huge ***Ta-daaah!***

Justine, our daughter, played *How much can I do to make sure I get an A?* She stayed after classes for study groups, did the extra credit, always did her homework, planned for, and started, projects weeks ahead of time. She even got help from others, including me when she needed it, which was seldom. She got straight A's, never once a B, and took college prep courses. She earned a full-ride scholarship to college. She also excelled in dance and played the same *How much can I do?* game there to become the best dancer in her class and competitions. Another phenomenal ***Ta-daaah!!!!!!***

Two smart kids, two high achievers, two people Trisha and I are proud of. And two kids who saved us from paying a lot of tuition money. Playing the right game can benefit others, too . . . like us 😊. Trisha is also a *How much can I do?* person in school, at work, in helping others. She has a way of having three or four bigger things that she plays the *How much can I do?* game with. As for me, I cap out at a couple of big initiatives: business and family.

Which brings me to my next point: This game we play can get out of balance if you aren't careful. You can't play the *How much can I do?* game with everything. You don't have an endless amount of time, money, or energy to spend. You must pick and choose what's important to you when deciding to play each game. When I'm cleaning our kitchen, something not so important to me, I'm playing the *How little can I do?* game and it's still *mostly* clean and my wife doesn't notice I skipped some areas. Sorry, honey . . . I told you this book would be revealing in so many ways. I don't play as many sports since I've gotten older, but I still like to mix it up on the golf course or tennis court. Now, when I play the *How much can I do?* game, I replace sports with work/business. It's how I compete and, if I'm anything, I'm competitive.

What's interesting about this game is that someone can start off playing the *How much can I do?* game but shift to playing the *How little can I do?* game over time. At work, some of our best technicians, salespeople, CSRs, and other positions are often our newest employees. They come into the organization with something to prove. They want to impress. They want to make their mark, setting themselves up for possible future promotions. They follow our system to a T. They don't skip steps and they often don't have bad habits (or enough of them to be a problem) and they rise to the top very quickly. They play the *How much can I do?* game.

Fast forward three or four years. These same individuals have often gravitated closer to mediocrity. They're still above average, but they have their own systems now and they skip the steps that drove their success, talking themselves into believing they're not always necessary. They've regressed into playing the *How little can I do and still be successful?* game. You can hear them say things like, "Yeah I used to do that, and still do when I need to." When I need to? What happened to doing something *all the time* if it works?

Why did these superstars decline? Why do some of the best performers in any organization reduce themselves to being merely average? They gravitate to playing *How little can I do and still make the sale?* They still make a decent number of sales because they are very skilled, but they're no longer exceptional. They're *comfortable*. And some may not adapt to changing conditions in the market, to competition, or to how consumers want to be sold. I hear them say things like, "I'm not doing anything different." That's normally not true, but even if it were, why wouldn't you do something different if it meant being more successful?

Think of the people you work with. You can probably put them in the two game buckets very quickly. And everyone else at work would probably put those employees in the same buckets you did. It's not a secret. It's not hard to see. It's easy to tell which game they're playing.

Can you imagine this *How little can I do?* philosophy in professional sports? You see it all the time. How little can I do in boxing out and still get the rebound in basketball? How little can I block and still protect the quarterback? If a team isn't good at blocking and tackling, the fundamentals, it's usually a function of playing the *How little can I do?* game. *How little can I practice and still win the game this week, going through the motions, but not giving it my best?* Ever notice that many sports stars credit their win to the fact they had a good week of practice and preparation? It's how upsets happen and underdogs win: When the clear favorite relaxes enough to play the wrong game.

Most everyone plays the *How much can I do?* game with something. It might not be work-related, but they surely are playing at a high level with some aspect of their life. It might be being a great dad or mother, wife or husband, grandparent, running a charity, pursuing a hobby, sports, a passion, working out, competing in something, church, politics, entertaining, and the list goes on. There are important things outside of work that are worth playing the *How much can I do?* game with. Hopefully it's not an addiction, a bad habit, something illegal, or something abusive. The game of *How much can I do?* can be a negative and dangerous when used the wrong way.

At work we talk about the two games and are open about which one each of us is playing. Recognize it. Call it out. Guard against *How little can I do?* and reward *How much can I do?*

It seems when people start making an amount of money they're comfortable with, or more money than they ever dreamed of making, they can easily slip into playing the wrong game. *Success can breed complacency.*

The tragedy of life is often not in our failure, but rather in our complacency; not in our doing too much, but rather in our doing too little; not in our living above our ability, but rather in our living below our capacities. —Benjamin E. Mays

And from one of one of the greatest coaches of all time, and personally one of my favorite quotes (I carried it in my wallet for years) . . .

Remember this your lifetime through:
Tomorrow there will be more to do.
And failure waits for all who stay
With some success made yesterday.
Tomorrow you must try once more,
And even harder than before
—John Wooden

Play the right game for the things that matter most. How much can I do to make sure I am a great parent, child, sibling, or friend? Be the very best salesperson, technician, installer, cleric, dispatcher, maintenance worker, employee, or entrepreneur that you can be. Or be the best leader you can be at work, in your church, as a coach, teacher, mentor, or any position of authority or influence. If you've fallen into the trap of playing the *How little can I do and still be successful?* game, reverse it. Play the game that assures you of your success in all endeavors: *How much can I do to make sure I'm as successful as I can be?* It doesn't guarantee you will win every time, but it gives you your best chance. And win or lose, you'll walk away from each call, each meeting, each presentation, each encounter with your kids or spouse every day knowing you gave it your all. Let your definition of success be, "I played the right game and I did my very best!"

Pulling Back the Curtain

★   One of our most successful salespeople had a routine on every sales call. He would park around the corner before he went to the call, clear his mind of any negative thoughts, go through the steps of our sales process, and visualize shaking hands and making the sale. Only then would he pull up to the customer's home. He played the *How much can I do?* game on every call. It's a great routine that's used by a lot of athletes and it can work for you, too.

★   What do you play the *How little can I do?* game with that someone important to you wishes you weren't? It's a good question to ask yourself, but maybe more importantly, to ask them.

★   *There is no elevator to success, you have to take the stairs.*
   —Zig Ziglar

My Fifth Trick

Getting Everyone on the Same Page

LOTS OF BOOKS AND SEMINARS talk about how important it is for your company to have a mission statement and a set of core values, to communicate them to everyone, post them on the wall, talk about them, and even memorize them. Some companies even recite them at the start of every meeting. I applaud those companies and leaders who make their mission and core values an integral part of their company.

Parker & Sons has a set of core values and a mission statement. They hang on the wall, and we occasionally bring them up or highlight them, but very few could recite them from memory, and they're certainly not interwoven into our day-to-day activities. Or are they? The fact of the matter is we *live* the core values and mission in everything we do. It's who we are. And even though we don't highlight it, *we still live it.* That's the important part. If someone described your culture or values, without ever seeing the poster, how would they describe your company? *That* is your mission statement and core values, no matter what hangs on the wall.

Parker & Sons SPIRIT Values

Service – we aim to provide the highest level of customer service.

Performance – we strive for excellence in everything we do.

Integrity – we are transparent and honest in our actions, and we adhere to ethical business practices.

Respect – we treat each other with dignity and fairness. Personal advancement is related to personal performance.

Innovation – we embrace creative solutions that improve our effectiveness.

Teamwork – through team effort, we translate individual efficiency into superior company performance.

Our Mission Statement is simple . . .

Be a great place to work
+ Provide World Class Service
= Grow the Business

Having a set of core values and a mission statement is a good step to creating your company culture, but demonstrating and living a mission and a set of core values is what's most important. It's what begins the process of getting everyone on the same page.

Themes can work as well. Themes are usually changed on yearly basis and it's popular to introduce them during annual kickoff meetings, but they can surface at any time if you put a little thought and energy into it. Themes can be unique to your company, or you can steal them shamelessly from others.

Last year's theme was *Can't Stop . . . Won't Stop.* We borrowed it from one of our premier manufacturers and partners who had used it a few years earlier and we kicked it off at our all-company meeting accompanied by Miley Cyrus's song, "We Can't Stop." Our keynote speaker was Aron Ralston, author of *Between a Rock and a Hard Place* which was adapted into the film *127 Hours*. It's one of the most moving stories I've ever heard. In April 2003, while descending alone into Bluejohn Canyon, he dislodged a boulder which pinned his hand against the canyon wall. A hundred and twenty-seven hours later, deprived of food and water, he was able to free himself by amputating his forearm with a dull knife and then hiking seven miles to safety. If you've never seen the movie or read the book, you're missing something truly remarkable.

We drove our theme home in several ways during the meeting and it became our battle cry throughout the year. We didn't have to push it much; it kind of just took off. Aron helped us do that in a big way. When someone was doing well, we heard "Can't Stop . . . Won't Stop." When someone wasn't doing well, we heard "Can't Stop . . . Won't Stop." It's one of those sayings that can be used in almost any situation. With 2020 being the year of COVID-19, we couldn't have picked a better battle cry. We didn't let anything, not even a pandemic, stop us from being successful.

This year's theme is *We Got This*. The virtual meeting was kicked off with a theme song, "I Got This," by country singer Jerrod Niemann. It's always good to have a catchy song to drive the theme home. Our keynote speaker was Mark Matteson, an ex-HVAC technician turned trainer and public speaker. Mark has been a mentor to some of the biggest names in the home-services business and he's one of the best trainers and speakers our industry has to offer. He helps train our leadership team and has made a big difference to many companies. He, like Aron, captivated his audience with life lessons, but unlike Aron, seasoned them with a lot of humor. His central theme was *Thinking Differently*.

 Themes and all-company meetings to kick off a year, a contest, or an initiative, can be very powerful. I learned that from the Wrench Group, now our parent company. They help us set up the new year and what we want to celebrate from the previous one.

Now I started this section not as a chapter, but as a "trick." So far, no trick. Well, hang on . . . I've always got one up my sleeve. Here it is: My trick to getting everyone on the same page, whether they want to be or not. Now it doesn't work with everyone, but it will work with over ninety-five percent of your audience or company. I've been in a room of four hundred people and had all but maybe fifteen of them on the same page, all thinking the same thing, on their own, simultaneously.

How does it work? Clear your mind. Concentrate for two minutes. And don't read on to the next step until you finish the previous one. Let's get started . . .

Think of a number between one and nine.

Got it? This step is the hardest part. It's okay to use a calculator.

Multiply your number by nine.

Got the result? Add the digits of that number together (If your result is eighteen, add one and eight).

You with me?

Now subtract five from that number

Got the result?

Now assign a letter of the alphabet to the number you just got: 1=A, 2=B, 3=C, and so on.

Got the letter?

Now think of a country that starts with that letter.

Almost there, I promise you.

Now take the last letter of that country's name and think of an animal that starts with that letter.

Last step: Take the last letter in the spelling of that animal and think of a color that starts with that letter.

Got it?

Turn the page . . .

Anyone thinking of Orange Kangaroos in Denmark?

See, we're all thinking the same. Wasn't that easy? And if you happen to be part of the five percent or so that had a different answer, that's ok. You like to follow the road less traveled, you're an independent thinker, you're well-versed in geography and foreign countries . . . or maybe need to brush up on your times tables ☺.

Ta-daaah!!!!!!!!

 Pulling Back the Curtain

★   I ran across this verse maybe thirty years ago and I've kept it ever since. It's a cute rendition of what can happen in some companies when you have a confusing mission statement, don't listen to your employees, or when leadership ignores issues. I thought it was appropriate here, especially since this trick is called "Getting Everyone on the Same Page."

The Plan

In the beginning there was a plan,
And then came the assumptions,
And the assumptions were without form,
And the plan without substance,

And the darkness was upon the face of the workers,
And they spoke among themselves, saying,
"It is a crock of shit and it stinks."

And the workers went unto their supervisors and said,
"It is a pile of dung and we cannot live with the smell."

And the supervisors went unto their managers, saying,
"It is a container of excrement and it is very strong,
Such that none may abide by it."

And the managers went unto their directors, saying,
"It is a vessel of fertilizer and none may abide by its strength."

And the Directors spoke among themselves, saying to one another,
"It contains that which aids plants growth and it is very strong."

And the directors went to the vice presidents, saying unto them,
"It promotes growth and it is very powerful."

And the vice presidents went to the president, saying unto him,
"This new plan will actively promote the growth and vigor
Of the company with very powerful effects."

And the president looked upon the plan
And saw that it was good,
And the plan became policy.

And this, my friend, is how shit happens.

Author unknown

Chapter Eleven

Marketing Success . . . The CliffsNotes

Doing business without advertising is like winking at a girl in the dark. You know what you are doing, but no one else does.
—**Steuart Henderson Britt**

I STARTED IN ACCOUNTING AFTER COLLEGE, and I've worked in operations, but my passion is marketing and advertising. I love the creative angle and, quite frankly, it's what my son and daughter are good at, so it's fun to toss ideas around with them. Here's some inside magic that has helped drive Parker & Sons' growth.

 The 1ˢᵗ Lesson I learned

There are three things in marketing and advertising that work flawlessly: *Consistency, Longevity,* **and** *Diversity.*

The same message (consistency), over a long period of time (longevity), over several media (diversity), nearly always works. If you're missing one of those elements, and especially if you're missing two, it just won't work as well, and maybe not at all. If you're on TV, radio, billboard, and the internet (diversity), but aren't consistent with your messaging, or if you only do it for three months, it normally won't work well. Many contractors, home-service providers, and small businesses don't understand this. They often lack marketing savvy. I would argue that some of the national brands aren't any better, so how could the typical contractor or small business, some small, ten-truck operation in Cincinnati, Ohio, be good at it? They usually aren't. They tend to bounce in and out of TV, radio, billboard, print, you name it, and never get the consistency, longevity, and diversity it takes to be successful.

Contractors, and many companies in all kinds of businesses, conclude that none of the traditional advertising works and they all end up in the same place where everyone else competes: in Google pay-per-click (PPC). There, every day, every company starts off at the same place, on a relatively level playing field, competing for clicks. And the click that used to cost five dollars for certain keywords now sometimes costs fifty, seventy-five, or a hundred dollars depending on the time of year and supply/demand.

These three ingredients are the secret to successful advertising and building a brand or message which can resonate with consumers and be remembered. However, the problem with consistency, longevity, and diversity, is that it's *expensive* and exceeds what the average contractor can afford. That used to be a disadvantage for our company, too, but now it's the one big advantage we have.

If you're large enough and have a big enough budget, you don't necessarily even have to be *good* at marketing and advertising. People will think you know what you're doing even if you don't. And because you're spending enough it can still work. Now, it's better if you're also good at what you do, but if you must make a choice of being good at marketing with a very small budget, or having a huge budget to spend but poor marketing talent, choose the latter. A larger budget will make everything work better.

Luckily, at our company we now have both: a big budget and marketing expertise. It's our big advantage. My son, Josh, handled the advertising until about five years ago when he started his own company, Clover Marketing, which caters to contractors that seek to grow their businesses. Like clover, which can take over a yard once it takes root, Clover Marketing (www.GrowWithClover.com) teaches its clients how to dominate a market. He and Laura, his wife, are one of our industry's premier marketing and sales-driven support teams. Their bite-sized "Jam Sessions," which are part of their "Contractor Catapult" program, are an affordable way for any contractor or small business to learn from the very best.

Meanwhile, at Parker & Sons, my daughter Justine took over from her brother and has also grown into one of the best marketers in our industry. She's a unique combination of being very creative, hardworking, and a great thinker about anything business or marketing related. Since she joined us five years ago we've almost tripled in size, growing up to thirty million dollars annually. She's made many key improvements in marketing and customer retention to help toward that cause. We seem to feed off of each other, constantly learning and perfecting the art of marketing and advertising.

I say this proudly about both of my kids and with no bias 😊. You'd need only look at our growth over the last seventeen years to know that someone in our family has a knack for marketing.

The 2nd Lesson I Learned

It's better to be a big fish in a small pond than a small fish in an ocean of advertisers.

Small fish in the ocean either get eaten or spend their lives swimming for cover. The strategy small fish use in the ocean—swarming very close together within a school to make themselves look like one large fish—won't work in the marketplace. No small contractor sticks together with several others, in any organized way, long enough to look big. Whatever you do, you must dominate it.

Within the Wrench Group, the group our company is now a part of, is a Dallas company called Baker Brothers. Jimmie, the president, uses a strategy of restricting advertising to two days a week. During those two days, though, you're going to see or hear him several times on TV and radio. I have friends who live in Dallas. Lennox, a key manufacturing partner of ours, is located there. Everyone I know in the Dallas-Fort Worth area thinks Baker Brothers ads run all week in all media. They've become top-of-mind in their market by collapsing their scheduled run days and being a bigger fish only on Tuesdays and Wednesdays.

In the early days, after buying Parker & Sons, we employed a similar strategy of dominating a small cable network of around a hundred thousand homes. We had negotiated a cost of just three dollars per spot back then versus fifty dollars or more on the much larger cable network. Our TV budget was only four thousand a month. We couldn't afford more. Thirteen hundred commercials running across several channels to a hundred thousand households works significantly better than eighty commercials running on larger footprint. Whatever you do, dominate it, even if it's to a smaller audience. You can do this by zoning cable, by choosing less-popular radio stations (but ones that still fit your demographic), or by targeting neighborhoods with local ads, direct mail, social media, and any number of other ways.

If you're large enough to dominate the ocean you now have a huge competitive advantage. But beware of showing any weakness: Even a big fish can be eaten.

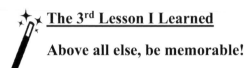

The 3rd Lesson I Learned

Above all else, be memorable!

I don't believe exposure on TV, radio, and print is automatically good exposure. I don't believe that any publicity is good publicity. There are plenty of companies that get caught doing the wrong thing. You might see one on the news in a sting operation. Or maybe it isn't even a bad company, they might just have a dishonest technician. No matter what someone might tell you, that's not the exposure you want. That said, there is some truth that consumers, and people in general, have short memories. And one of the most important objectives of advertising is to be memorable.

A professionally produced, well-made commercial only counts when the creative aspect (what people in the business call *the creative*) is memorable. Otherwise, all you really have is a nice-looking car that sits in the garage and never gets driven. If you're a collector of cars, or of "great production quality" commercials, good for you. For me, it's all about *Can this creative make the phone ring or drive people to my website?* That's what counts.

Many companies, even large ones, have bland, boring commercials. They say things like, "Most trusted company . . .," "We care about . . .," "Quality service . . .," "Affordable pricing . . .," and the most famous of all meaningless claims, "Satisfaction guaranteed . . .," Everybody says these things. More importantly, any competitor can claim them, too. They aren't unique, and they are rarely backed up with any kind of meat on the bone. Satisfaction guaranteed *or what?* What happens if I'm not satisfied? ". . . or your money back" comes to mind, and it's better than nothing, but maybe still too generic. Of course I'm going to get my money back if you can't deliver what you sold me. Be memorable. For a pest-control company, *"Satisfaction guaranteed or we'll eat a bug"* would be excellent. I can remember that one 😊.

The 4ᵗʰ Lesson I Learned

Marketing and advertising are constantly evolving. You must adapt.

What worked years ago might not work now. The demographic of your customer base can change over time. As with many other products and services, the move to booking and selling online is evolving. Online sales now account for close to twenty percent of all U.S. retail sales. The recording TV shows to watch later has changed some strategies in marketing, regarding what shows to advertise on and how to counteract the fast-forwarding habits of viewers. Streaming shows are on the rise, especially with younger demographics. Social media and online marketing influencers are more popular than ever. People want to buy online more and interact less. Booking a call online versus calling in is certainly a trend in our industry and many others as well.

More is changing than staying the same. And the rate of change is accelerating. That's good news for those who can adapt, and really bad news for those who can't or won't. Each of the above as an opportunity to learn how to get better and outperform the competition.

The 5ᵗʰ Lesson I Learned

Be different and stand for something.

What does your company stand for? What do you want consumers to remember about your company? What is your differentiator?

It can be an offer or feature/benefit, but it's better when it's a feeling or emotion.

Justine and I once helped a sizable company that had been struggling to grow at the rate they wanted. They had averaged mid-single-digit growth but wanted to figure out how to grow twenty percent or more. We asked the president and marketing manager, *What do you want consumers to remember about your company?* Simple question, right? But they hadn't thought about marketing that way. Most contractors don't. They were advertising generic slogans, like in the 3rd lesson above, but they didn't have anything memorable, or something that differentiated them from their competition. Their TV, radio, and billboards were professional, but not memorable.

At Parker & Sons, we originally created a character that people could relate to: "Melvin," the sloppy service tech that no one wants in their home. Melvin was the antithesis of what a good tech should be. We would say and show how we were different than Melvin, and then ended each commercial with our slogan: "There'll be no Melvins on your job." To make it a positive commercial, we exaggerated what Melvin did, and used humor to make it fun and memorable. Melvin was almost going out of his way to say and do stupid but entertaining things. It wasn't long before we realized we had a winner. We heard consumers talking about their husband being *a real Melvin* when it comes to home projects. We even had an occasional complaint that Melvin was someone's family name and they'd appreciate it if we would take the commercials off the air.

Our new creative is about "Joe," a tech who fixes what you need fixed, but then does something for the customer that you'd never expect a tech to do, from cooking dinner to getting the kids back to sleep, after the AC goes out in the middle of the night. Joe is everything you'd want in a tech and then some. All the commercials end with the slogan, "Parker & Sons! We're not your average Joe." Humor is a great angle in stressful situations (like being without AC, hot water, or electricity).

My favorite advertising book, one that outlines what works and how to draw on consumers' emotions, is *Sheep Don't Eat Complicated Grass*, by Brian Gregory. It takes a restaurant and shows you, in very simple terms (the only kind I understand), how to draw out an emotional response from the reader based on ad design, the graphics, and the phrasing. It's a brilliant book, even if you aren't in the restaurant business. The concepts apply to any business. Brian helped us for a short sprint with some of the creative work at our company and he's a good resource for anyone's think tank.

The 6th Lesson I Learned

Build a good online reputation.

In the old days, referrals happened across a fence, neighbor-to-neighbor, or at the beauty salon, friend-to-friend. Referrals still happen this way, but they seem to occur less and less. People are busy these days and neighbors don't see or talk to neighbors like they used to. Nowadays, the garage door goes up, the car pulls in, and the garage door goes down. I can go months without talking to a neighbor, sad but true. Or you might not even know your neighbor well enough to trust them as a good referral source for a home project, a doctor, a car issue, or even a restaurant.

What's taken the place of face-to-face referrals are online referral services like Angie's List, Home Advisor, or here in Phoenix, MyGuy Referrals. A more prominent quasi-referral is online reviews: reviews from people you don't know, don't necessarily trust, and some potentially from competitors, or even from the company that's being reviewed. You have to read a lot of them to get a sense of how good a company is.

With all the inherent flaws, online reviews are very influential in consumers' buying decisions. Your star rating on Google, Facebook, BBB, Angie's List, and Yelp can be what makes someone hire you . . . or not. The reviews and what they say about you also become part of your online reputation.

The number of reviews you have is also important. A 4.9-star rating for a company with ten reviews is not nearly as impressive or reliable as a 4.7-star rating for a company with five thousand reviews. Regardless of how you manage your online reputation, make sure to address negative reviews right away. Showing that you care enough to reply and make things right can snuff out those bad reviews before they do any real damage.

That's my CliffNotes version of marketing and advertising. There is so much more we could get into. We've learned so much over the years, and we continue to learn today. With what we spend in advertising, we can afford to experiment a bit and test different strategies. We aren't marketing geniuses, but we're pretty good at it. Over the years, we've learned what works and, just as importantly, what doesn't. You've heard the phrase *If at first you don't succeed, try, try again.*

I'd like to change it slightly.

If at first, you don't succeed, don't tell anyone.

Advertising can be like that. People think we're geniuses at marketing and advertising. They don't know how much money we've spent on things that didn't work. I hope I've saved you a little trial and error in this chapter.

Oh, I almost forgot this one last piece of good advice . . .

If at first you don't succeed, don't try skydiving.

👤 Pulling Back the Curtain

★ The above are all great lessons, but the greatest marketing lesson of all, one that will give you an advantage, is "think like your customer." Customers are not as complicated as we sometimes make them out to be. Marketing that is clear, simple, interesting, meaningful, impactful, and entertaining is what customers want.

★ We buy on emotion and justify with logic. Appealing to emotion is critical. One of the best books I've read on advertising and how to appeal to a consumer's emotions is Brian Gregory's *Sheep Don't Eat Complicated Grass*. Get yourself a copy, but finish this book first 😊.

★ *The best place to hide a dead body is on page two of Google search results.* —Anonymous

Chapter Twelve

Selling a Grudge Purchase

Give me the luxuries of life and I will willingly do without the necessities.
—**Frank Lloyd Wright**

THIS TITLE OF THIS CHAPTER MIGHT NOT PERTAIN TO THE BUSINESS YOU OWN OR WORK FOR, or the products or services you sell, but the concepts in it still apply. The business of HVAC, plumbing, and electrical maintenance, repairs, and installations, is mostly an emergency-based business, and a *grudge purchase*. No one woke up today excited about buying a new air conditioner or water heater, or counting the minutes until the electrician arrives to rewire their house. These are "have-to" purchases made with money you'd rather spend elsewhere. They're grudge purchases.

Much of the home-services industry is based on needs that arise quickly and need to be taken care of on the same day. Your AC is out in July in Phoenix, your heat is out in January in Minneapolis, water is pouring through your ceiling or bubbling up from your floor, you have no hot water, or your toilet won't flush; your electric is out, or your refrigerator keeps blowing a fuse. You discover a mouse in your pantry, a snake in your garage, or termites in your walls. Your pool pump died and twenty-four kids are on their way over for a birthday party. All your plants are dying because your irrigation system stopped working. Your roof is leaking and the rain is ruining your carpet and furniture. Your car won't start or, worse, won't stop.

If all these are happening simultaneously I'd suggest you move back in with your parents. Doesn't sound appealing? Then call our company, Parker & Sons.

All kidding aside, these things do happen and, when they do, it's an emergency. Speed of service is paramount. But it's also a grudge purchase. No one wants these things to happen, and very few are proactive enough to do what's needed to *prevent* them from happening.

When it comes to these types of services, nearly everyone waits for something to happen before making a purchase. The event triggers the pain or discomfort of being *without* those things. Getting consumers to invest in a new air conditioner or water heater before they have to (and when they really *should*) is hard. Getting good at this is paramount to a company's success, and many times the company's existence. If you own an AC company and are only busy when it's blazing hot, when "events" are being triggered for you, you're going to have issues the other seven months of the year. You must find a way to get consumers to buy your products or services *before* the event happens.

Most contractors, when trying to talk someone into buying early, before the event, try to create future pain by creating a picture of what will happen if your air goes out next summer when you have company in from out-of-town, or if your roof leaks when the monsoons hit. Examples of future pain are easy to create, but very hard to feel. Can you effectively create future pain for an event that may never happen? It's hard! Doctors can't even do it. They'll tell you that if you don't stop smoking, lose weight, eat right, exercise, you're at risk of developing cancer, having a heart attack, getting diabetes, or having hip and knee problems. Do we listen? Rarely. We have to *get* cancer, *have* heart disease, *the event has to happen,* and then we change our lifestyles (for at least a while).

If doctors can't create future pain, what makes us think *we* can? I'm not against conjuring in the consumer's mind what can and will happen in the future, I just don't think the pain is great enough to make them do anything prior to the event.

We teach our technicians and salespeople to create *current pain,* by reminding them of what they are already experiencing with their current AC system, water heater, or electrical panel: the pain of the air conditioner that doesn't keep you comfortable, the pain of playing the *thermostat game* where each spouses takes turns changing the temperature, the pain of paying an extra hundred dollars a month to the utility company when you could have used that money to make a monthly payment for a new system, the pain of the racket your old AC system makes outside your bedroom on hot summer nights, the pain of running out of hot water whenever you wash clothes and take a shower at the same time. People can feel current pain, if reminded, just like they feel it when they receive a doctor's bill or pay a huge deductible.

Future pain? Yes, but it's not that effective. Current pain? Yes, and it can be moderately effective. But the thing we have learned is that everything else pales in comparison to the pain of buying a new AC system, or water heater, or electrical panel. And the pain of buying those things isn't in the booking of the call, taking off work to be home, or the pain of what kind of tech will show up. There can be pain there, too, but with a good company, that pain is minimal.

The real pain is in spending the money to fix the problem or replace the thing that broke. It's painful to spend money for a new HVAC system that can run as high as fifteen thousand dollars, or a water heater that can run up to three thousand dollars. That's painful!

People avoid pain, they don't run to it. The trick to getting someone to consider buying something before an event rests in reducing or eliminating the pain of buying the thing you want them to buy. To do that, you need to make it affordable. If I've gotten you interested in all the advantages of a new HVAC system and then shocked you with a ten-thousand-dollar price you'd probably want to wait for your AC to go out before enduring that kind of pain. But, if it were only ninety-nine dollars a month—three dollars a day—and you tip that much for lunch, you might be way more interested. Three dollars a day is a small price to pay to

- be more comfortable in the home you and family spend half your lives in.
- have a quiet system (some are quieter than your refrigerator).
- stop playing the thermostat game with your spouse.
- cool off that room that's always too hot in the summer.
- have better air and cut down on germs, bacteria, and viruses.
- be environmentally friendly, using the new refrigerant.
- not worry about it breaking down on the year's hottest day.
- make your home worth more or sell faster.
- save close to a thousand dollars on your utility bill each year.

All that for ninety-nine dollars a month, or three dollars a day. Sounds like a bargain, doesn't it?

We call that the *net investment:* your monthly payment minus the monthly utility savings. The lesson in the above example is that we make it affordable, which lessens or eliminates the pain of buying, allowing people to make a decision that is truly best for themselves and their families. Once affordability is established, we need only establish urgency (*Why do this now?*) to get some customers to buy ahead of the eventual event. They know their AC could last a few more months or it could last a year more. If we can make it affordable why not replace it now?

░ Pulling Back the Curtain

★ This chapter is about *our* business, and certainly the examples used might not pertain directly to your business, but the thought process is a valuable lesson and will pertain to any business. What are the pain points within the purchasing decision for your customers? How can you reduce or eliminate them? What are your customers waiting for before they purchase your product or service? Can you give them what they want now vs. the risk of waiting? Can you create more pain when they don't move forward with a purchase than when they do? Are the benefits of your product or service great enough to offset the perceived value your customer assigns to the price you charge? Can you figure out how to provide more value, at a lower pain point or cost, than you currently offer?

My Sixth Trick

Getting Rid of the Hiccups in Life and Business

IN LIFE AND BUSINESS THERE ARE THINGS THAT DON'T GO RIGHT, things that can throw you off, and lots of unexpected challenges. Life certainly has its share of hiccups and bad news. If you aren't careful, they can ruin your mood, your perspective, a marriage, a relationship, a business. By living a certain kind of life, and reducing your risks, you can limit or mitigate how many bad things happen, or the severity of what happens, but you will still encounter setbacks, or what I like to call *hiccups*. As I've told my children, you're guaranteed to make mistakes, you just want to steer away from making the big ones or the same ones over and over. Regardless of how careful you are, what kind of life you lead, or how many procedures and safeguards your business might have in place, bad news will surely find you. This trick isn't about how to prevent bad news, but rather how to handle it.

We had an industry trainer named Rick Hutcherson who used to do training for our company. The first morning was all about resetting how you think and changing your perspective. He told the story of Bethany Hamilton who, while surfing, was attacked by a tiger shark. Some of you may have read her book (or seen the movie) *Soul Surfer: A True Story of Faith, Family, and Fighting to Get Back on the Board.*

On October 31, 2003, Bethany Hamilton, who was thirteen years old, went surfing with her best friend's family in Hawaii. A fourteen-foot-long tiger shark severed her left arm just below the shoulder. Her friend's family paddled her back to shore and made a tourniquet for her injured arm. By the time she arrived at the hospital she had lost over sixty percent of her blood and was in hypovolemic shock.

She lost her left arm but otherwise came through it all in good shape. One month after the attack, Bethany Hamilton was back on the board.

Her philosophy? *"I don't need easy, I just need possible."*

What Rick taught, which I always remembered, was that you can be a one-armed surfer and be happy, or you can be a one-armed surfer and be miserable . . . you're still a one-armed surfer. Likewise, you can go to work and be happy or you can go to work and be miserable . . . you're still going to work. You or a loved one can get cancer and be miserable, or you can figure out how to be happy anyway . . . you still have cancer. Happiness is a choice, not something that happens to you. Likewise, being miserable is a choice, not something that happens to you. *"Folks are usually about as happy as they make their minds up to be."* —Abraham Lincoln

Bad things happen and I don't want to downplay that. Nor do I want to ignore the stages people must go through when dealing with bad news, coping with life-changing health issues, losing a major account at work, getting laid off, dealing with a troubled teen, or any number of other bad hands life deals to you or, even worse, bad hands you deal to yourself. All are painful and can surely affect you, your family, your job, or your relationships. How you handle them is what matters.

My dad passed early from heart-related issues. He never complained once. My mom had blood cancer, multiple myeloma, and was in pain throughout her last years, especially in her final months. She never complained and was one of the happiest people I've known throughout her ordeal. My father-in-law, when dealing with kidney failure and on dialysis, never talked about it and never complained. My mother-in-law, still with us, has leukemia and deals with constant issues because of it, but she trudges along and maintains an upbeat attitude despite the challenges. "Getting old ain't for sissies" is how my father-in-law use to say it. My sisters and my brother-in-law have had multiple knee and hip surgeries and other ailments and have lived in pain for many years. Neither one complains . . . ever. Most people would. I admire those who never make their problem someone else's.

All these bad things can be show-stoppers and if you aren't careful they can define who you are. You can retreat into self-pity or into a life devoid of happiness. Or you figure out how to deal with them. Like the hiccups, the ill effects of bad news can go away, and most do over time. Even if they don't, you can still learn to deal with them, to adjust, to reset priorities, to live happily within the restrictions that life or business deals you.

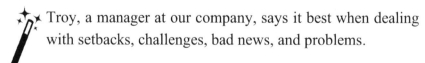 Troy, a manager at our company, says it best when dealing with setbacks, challenges, bad news, and problems.

Don't nurse it.
Don't curse it.
Don't rehearse it.
Just disperse it
And give it to God. He'll reverse it.

For me, this poem was a truly wonderful **Ta-daaah.** I added that last line based on a similar saying I had heard from a teacher. It's good advice. It's easy to take bad news and feed into it (nurse it), then get mad and share it with everyone (curse it), let it consume you, repeating it over and over in your mind (rehearse it), when all you really have to do (eventually anyway), is let it go (disperse it), and pray to God to help you with it.

We each have the power to take any circumstance, bad or good, and make the most of it. I'm reminded of a morning when I was in college and my dad asked me if I had fun the night before. My friends and I had gone to a new bar. It was kind of a dingy place, not very big, and wasn't very crowded. We didn't have a good time, which was unusual for my friends and me. We just hadn't seemed to be in the mood. I was complaining about the bar when my dad stopped me and said, "Son, it wasn't the bar. If you go anywhere with your friends, your family, or even yourself, and have a bad time, it's your own fault." *It's my own fault!* I knew he was right. It wasn't the bar; we just weren't in a partying mood. And, contrary to tradition, none of us broke out of the mood and lifted the others up.

That was a valuable lesson, and it still is. If you're in a bad mood, or down in the dumps, not enjoying life, not having fun at work, or not laughing enough, it's your own fault. You're in control of your mood, of your feelings, of whether or not you have fun, whether you laugh, and whether you're happy, no matter the circumstance. You control your thoughts and your thoughts control your life. Once you truly realize this you can be blessed with an enormous sense of peace knowing you'll be happy and enjoy life no matter what life might throw at you.

Here's the trick, it's a funny and practical ***Ta-daaah:*** How to get rid of hiccups. And I don't mean the bumps or hurdles in life. I mean the literal hiccups, the spasms you get when you eat too fast or too much, exercise, or drink too much on a Friday night (not that I'd know anything about that).

Hiccups are annoying and if they go on long enough (days), they can even be life threatening. Charles Osborn holds the Guinness World Record for the longest bout of hiccups. In 1922, he got the hiccups when a hog fell on him. Sixty-eight years later, in 1990, they finally stopped. True story! He hiccupped an estimated four hundred and thirty million times. Jennifer Mee, a teenager, has the record for most frequent hiccups, fifty times each minute for five weeks straight. Can you imagine?

There are many well-known methods to supposedly get rid of hiccups: holding your breath, breathing into a paper bag, drinking water upside down, scaring the hiccuppee (if that's a word), and sometimes these actually work, but there's one trick you probably haven't tried or even heard of.

While cleaning out the family attic many years ago, my mom ran into a recipe box her mother had stored away. Within it, among handwritten recipes for family meals, desserts, and appetizers, was an unusual item credited to Elsie, my grandmother's long-ago neighbor. It's reproduced on the next page . . .

<u>Recipe for Hiccups</u>

It's a tongue twister. Take one really big breath, and say five times real fast, along with the last line, in a southern accent (spelled how you should say it), and your hiccups will be cured.

Heecup, Teacup, Teacup, Heecup

Heecup, Teacup, Teacup, Heecup

Heecup, Teacup, Teacup, Heecup

Heecup, Teacup, Teacup, Heecup

Heecup, Teacup, Teacup, Heecup

Because Elsie told me so.

That alone is worth the price of this book. I've shared this trick with maybe fifty people and, with a few exceptions, it's worked. It requires no preparation or materials . . . no bag, no water, no cup, no scaring the begeebies out of someone. As a result, it's my "go to" hiccup cure. And because it reminds me of my mom, I personally get a kick out of sharing it. It's fun to see the reaction when I tell people about the cure and the story behind it, and to hear them attempt their southern twang when saying it. But I'm "tickled to death," as they say in the South, when they find out it works. Try it out the next time someone gets the hiccups.

Ta-daaah!

Pulling Back the Curtain

★ Happiness is a choice, not something that happens to you. You can choose to be happy no matter what life throws at you.

★ Learn from your pets. No matter what happened that day to little Buddy, our dog, he still jumped up on us as we came in the door each day, licked us, and wanted to play. He was excited to see us. Even when he was hurt or sick, he still seemed to be in a good mood. He chose, every day, to be happy. And pets, whether it's your dog, a cat, rabbit, bird, fish, or guinea pig, love you unconditionally and can snap you out of even the worst mood.

★ *Be happy. It really annoys negative people.* —Ricky Gervais

Chapter Thirteen

Revving Up Your Sales Engine

You will either step forward into growth, or you will step back into safety.
—**Abraham Maslow**

VIRTUALLY EVERY COMPANY EVENTUALLY RUNS INTO A SALES OR REVENUE PROBLEM. It can be economically driven, like a recession, or market driven. Declining sales can be weather driven for certain businesses. Government or local regulation changes can also affect growth, as can supply chain issues. We've seen how a pandemic can devastate some industries, while fueling others. A technological change can disrupt a business or industry, as can a new competitor. And internal issues, sometimes self-inflicted, can lead to falling revenue. There is no shortage of things that can affect the top line.

The story is always the same, though. Growth slows, and revenue flattens or declines. Often, without the right leadership, everyone can get good at the blame-game, operations pointing at marketing ("The creative is old and stale and the plan that used to work isn't any longer. We need better marketing"). Marketing points at sales ("We're just not closing the leads and we've lost our edge in the market. Our salespeople can't close a lead without taking a significant discount"). It's a vicious cycle when the revenue curve goes downhill.

Sound familiar? Hopefully not, but at some point most companies will go through it. When it happens, investors, leadership, and the board meet to discuss the options.

Options to help offset a revenue decline

1. Price Increase

Ah . . . the easiest answer to improving revenue short-term. This is the low-hanging fruit. We'll just charge a little more to help offset the revenue decline while we figure this out. A price increase is easy to implement, too, so it can be done very quickly.

Unfortunately, the easy answer isn't always best. The sales department complains that our pricing is already too high, and if you think we had trouble selling before, buckle up. Marketing is afraid consumers won't pay for the increase and we'll have trouble getting the phone to ring. Operations is afraid the price increase will have the opposite result that management is looking for.

2. Price Decrease

Yes!!! We need to get more competitive. If we discount more we can close more sales. Yes, we might not make as much on each sale, but we'll make it up in volume. We've all heard that one. I once heard a business owner say, "I might lose a little bit on each sale, but I'll make it up in volume." You don't have to be a math wizard to figure out where *that* strategy leads you. The sales department loves the idea, though. "Finally, they're listening!" The salespeople applaud and they know it's going to get a little easier to sell something. Or is it? Because what happens when you drop your price to beat the competition? Competition will respond in kind. We call that a *race to the bottom.*

3. Cost Cutting

Oh no, the dreaded cost cutting, first disguised as cost containment and probably only temporary, and later sometimes magnified to an "all unnecessary cost out" strategy and made permanent. If it doesn't produce revenue or profit we don't need to spend it.

Although everyone understands why cost-cutting is necessary, this decision is never popular. Sales doesn't like it. Operations just lost their capital-expenditure budget for new vans, so they're not loving it. And what normally accompanies any good cost-cutting mandate? The ever-popular hiring freeze. A freeze warning isn't just something you see on the Weather Channel. It's a cold, lonely place to be. And if it doesn't work, then we'll graduate to layoffs. Great! Now everyone gets to fear for their job. Although necessary in some circumstances, the cost-cutting route of offsetting falling sales is never popular.

Cost cutting often comes in the way of cutting the advertising budget. "We're spending money on advertising that, for whatever reason, isn't working. Why spend it? "Let's save the money and bring it to the bottom line." I hear that a lot. I sometimes end that last sentence at *bottom* because that's sometimes where the company is headed. But it does make sense that you shouldn't spend money on ineffective advertising. Unless, of course, you could find a way to *make* it work. That's the better answer.

I have a term I use when I see cost cutting become too harmful: *corporate anorexia*. Corporate anorexia sets in when the cost cutting lasts too long, is too widespread, or is too deep. The company, division, or location becomes so weak from the cuts tearing at the fabric of what once made it successful. Morale is low and everyone has lost confidence in the leadership, a sure sign of a company's demise. The company is so weak they couldn't grow if they wanted to.

Now I'm not against strategic cost-cutting. Sometimes it's necessary. But make sure you have a plan to get back to growth as soon as possible.

4. Driving Revenue

There is another way out, but it's not without risks. Before I get into it, I need to tell you a real-life story.

I'm not a boater. I love riding on them, but I've never owned one, never took care of one, and have rarely driven one. I'm all about knowing *someone else* who has a boat. I've heard too many boat owners repeat that famous line: *The happiest two days in a boat owner's life are the day he buys the boat and the day he sells it.* That said, I once learned a very valuable lesson from a boat owner.

Bob loved to race boats. He was out one day on his friend's boat. There were three of them on board, racing in a competition on a lake in northern California. During the race, they hit a large wave and the boat came down hard, cracking the transom in the back of the boat. The engine stopped running and the boat was taking on water. There they were, out of the race, in the middle of a large lake, in a sinking boat. They frantically grabbed whatever they could and started bailing as fast as they could, but the water was coming into it faster than they could bail.

That's when Bob had an idea. He jumped into the driver's seat, put it in neutral, turned the key and, sure enough, the engine turned over. The motor was fine, it had just stalled out. He put it in forward and picked up speed as the other two men bailed more slowly. As he gained speed and the boat levelled out, the water in the boat drained. They radioed ahead and went to the dock where they were able to save the boat and themselves.

When I heard that story I realized it really wasn't a boat story at all. It was a perfect example of what a company needs to do to stay out of trouble, avoid the need for cost-cutting, or, if it does get into profit difficulties, how to get out of it. The bailing of water was all the energy and effort toward cost cutting, the layoffs, the focus of some companies on how to cut or reduce losses. Bob starting the engine up is the answer for any company. The sales engine needs to be a fine-tuned machine. It needs to be able to run hard when needed, and it always has to keep you moving forward. And if it ever stalls out, someone needs to jump up in the driver's seat and get it started again, pull away from your troubles, and get your organization back on the level so you can get it to safety, meaning growth and profitability.

I started this chapter saying this method doesn't come without risks. What if I spend extra time, money, and energy to drive revenue and it doesn't work? I'll be in even worse shape. It's sometimes easier to play it safe, but it's rarely better. You need the right plan and the right people in the right places to turn around. If you don't, hire or get some help from outside. Never stop tweaking your marketing and advertising, getting crazy good at answering the phone, converting online leads, making more out of every customer interaction, and all the things we've talked about, which translates into strong revenue growth.

☝ Pulling Back the Curtain

★ At Parker & Sons we have a small group that has a simple barometer of our success in driving revenue. It's become sort of a funny but simple way of looking at our success. Our CFO, Erika, started a chart where we track our monthly revenue and plot it graphically, year to year. You can then easily see how a particular month compares with current-year months and, more importantly, how it compares with the same month in the previous year. The months are then connected linearly. Our mantra is simple: *Don't let the lines touch*, meaning *Don't have a month which is the same or less than the previous year*. That's it. That's all I care about. *Don't let the lines touch.* We've gone five years in a row without a touch. Now we have budgets and goals and a lot of measurements, but this one is my personal favorite. If you own a company, are in sales, on commission, earn tips, or are in any position where you have revenue or production goals, <u>don't let your lines touch!</u>

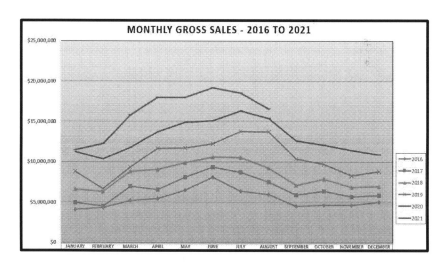

Don't let your lines touch!

117

Chapter Fourteen

The War for Talent

There's only one thing worse than training your staff and having them leave, and that's not training them and having them stay.
—**Zig Zigler**

IN THE HOME SERVICE INDUSTRY, especially in the contractor arena, there is a war going on. It's not a war *against* someone, it's a war *for* someone. It's the war for *talent*. In our industry, the greatest battle is for technicians and installers. Many businesses and industries are fighting the same war for programmers, nurses, doctors, waitresses, chefs, salespeople, engineers, mechanics, truck drivers, teachers, telemarketers, and so on. It's not just a war to fill the seats needed for demand or growth, but to fill the positions with the best talent in that industry.

I traveled the country for years helping contractors grow their businesses and improve profitability. One question I always asked was, "What is one thing that is stopping you from growing more?" Almost without exception, every owner responded the same way: "I could grow a lot faster if only I could find and hire good technicians." The Bureau of Labor Statistics recently reported an average expected job growth of fourteen percent over the next decade for HVAC technicians, plumbers, and electricians, compared with only five percent for other industries. At the same time, most people in the trades are expected to retire or leave the industry in the next ten years, and younger workers seem less interested in skilled trades, so retirees won't be easily replaced.

There you have it. The biggest problem in our industry, and in many industries, is *finding, hiring, and retaining the best*. When you think about it, in virtually any service industry of any kind, how well you hire and retain exceptional employees will ultimately determine the fate of your company. To the customer, those who deliver the service *are* your company or business.

My wife and I frequent certain restaurants, not always because of the exceptional food, but because of the exceptional person who serves us. They make you feel special and you have fun with them. You might be okay with so-so food as long as the experience is enjoyable. Our daughter waitressed for years and got the most tips of anyone that restaurant ever had. Why? It wasn't because the food was exceptional. It wasn't even that it was prepared quickly, or that the restaurant had great ambience. None of that was the case, and tips are usually never about any of that. She got great tips because she was always in a great mood, took an interest in the customer, made them laugh, had fun, *and* provided exceptional service too.

What struck me as I traveled from company to company was that everyone could identify this problem, everyone knew it held them back, everyone seemed to jump to complaining about it, but no one spent any real time, effort, or money solving it. The most important thing a leader, manager, or supervisor could do—finding, hiring, and retaining the best—was the very thing they spent the least amount of time doing, and not by a little—by a *lot*. I used to ask owners and managers what activity they used to hire and retain the best

119

people. In my head, I'd add up the minutes or hours it took them to do that activity. I rarely got past a full day of activity in a month. Not even eight hours in a whole month? Sometimes it was only minutes. If you wanted to learn a language, and only spent a few minutes every month on it, how fluent would you be after a year? Not very! So we talk ourselves into just learning the essentials, like "gracias," "sí," "cómo está," "muy bien," "baños," and "una mas cerveza, por favor." If that's the measure of learning a language, I'm fluent in Spanish.

How do you win the war for talent?

 ### Spend more time, money, and energy on it.

It's that simple! And meeting often enough, with the right people (Remember Trick #2?), can help force you to spend more time, money, and energy on it. When I do training I always do an exercise on this subject. The exercise is revealing in many ways. I'll use a group of contractors as my example.

Referral Fee Exercise

Think of your best technician, the one the customers love. He does great work, he's honest, hardworking, works when we need him, doesn't complain, is a high producer, and everyone at work loves it when he shows up.

Now everyone stand up and remain standing until I get to an amount of money that you *wouldn't* pay in a referral fee, sign-on bonus, or advertising, to get a tech just like that. And you have to assume he or she stays with you for a long time. When I get to an amount you wouldn't pay, sit down.

Who would pay a thousand dollars for a guy like that? *Everyone's standing.*

How about two thousand? *Everyone's usually still standing.*

Five thousand? Who would pay five thousand dollar? *Some, maybe even most, have sat down.*

I'll get crazy now and jump to ten thousand dollars. Who would be willing to pay ten thousand? *Virtually everyone is sitting.*

Just for fun, and since there are only a handful still standing, who would be crazy enough to pay twenty thousand dollars? *Sometimes everyone sits down on this one, but usually there are two or three still up (in a room of a hundred or more).*

I'll call on one of them. So you would actually pay twenty thousand dollars for someone like that?

They answer Yes.

Why? *I ask. They normally respond with something like,* Because he'd pay for himself, and cover that investment, in a matter of a couple months.

I wrap up the exercise like this:

Sometimes it doesn't even take months. It might only take weeks, and sometimes, if they are really good, only days for you to recoup your investment. And I applaud you for calling it an *"investment"* because that really does sum it up perfectly. It's an investment, much like training is. Now you don't have to spend twenty thousand dollars to get a good guy, but the idea that you *could* is the real point of the exercise. Don't pigeonhole your thinking and limit yourself into what you can spend in money, time, or effort to find, recruit, hire, and retain the best. It's an investment that will pay off for years and you almost can't spend enough to make sure you get it right and have all the best people in your industry.

At the beginning of this chapter I called it a *war*, and in the contractor trades, it is certainly that. Some competitors have taken the above exercise to heart, advertising five-thousand-dollar sign-on bonuses. One offers a ten-thousand-dollar sign-on bonus, a brand-new truck, tickets to sporting events, paid vacations, and the craziness goes on-and-on. In the end, if you must buy your way to hiring the best, and that's all you've got, you're probably not the best company to work for. That said, some technicians can follow the money. It reminds me of something Rick Hutcherson, a trainer in our industry that I mentioned earlier in the book, preached:

> *If you chase money, money will run from you, and you will become its slave. If you chase a purpose, money will run to you, and it will become your slave.*

Great advice. Never chase money, let it chase you. It's common to see very smart businesspeople in the news because they or their company are in trouble from chasing the money. The best salesmen don't chase money, they chase what is truly best for the customer. I've seen many people lose much of their savings investing in a hot deal, some insider tip, or chasing a seemingly sure deal. Let your purpose be to become the best company to work for, and then spend enough time, money, and energy finding and hiring the best.

Next, in the training I do, I might go into all the tricks and methods we use to recruit, hire, and retain good people. We hire over two hundred and fifty new employees a year, so we've gotten pretty good at it. I say pretty good because it's still a struggle and can still be a challenge. I'm not going to go into all the things we've discovered, but I will highlight one in each category.

Recruiting

Birds of a feather flock together. Your current employees usually know people, or know people who know people, or can find ways to run into people. They can reach out to old friends, past co-workers, associations, neighbors, or anyone who might know of a good technician, CSR, accountant, admin, etc. Pay them a spiff for their efforts and don't be afraid to make it significant, per the above exercise. You can pay in increments with a certain amount when you hire someone, on amount after ninety days, and even more after a year. Referrals are a great lead source, but you must work at it.

Your employees or you, reaching out to former top-notch employees, is another referral angle. Many former employees realize that leaving was a mistake, but like many people, they're too proud to admit it. Them knowing how much they're missed will go a long way toward getting them to consider returning.

Hiring

Make hiring fun. Make it a big deal. Make them feel welcome. Make it easy to apply for a job and make sure someone talks to people who come in to apply. Have an orientation program. Exceptional training is paramount. A big brother or sister they can call on or who will take a special interest in helping them and making them feel welcomed is another good way to improve the onboarding process.

The hiring process is their first real impression of your company. Put a lot of time, money, and effort in making it a WOW experience. This is an area we're working on at our company right now. By the time you finish this book we're going to be better at it than we were before. As Mark Matteson says, "We don't need to be sick to get better!"

Retaining

As mentioned in various sections of this book, we spend three things in life: time, money, and energy. In the old days, money was important and time a bit less. It wasn't unusual for you, your parents, and your grandparents to work sixty hours a week, *every* week, until they physically couldn't. In our industry, HVAC technicians, plumbers, and electricians tend to be younger. I mean, who wants to be in a sweltering attic in June, or in a ditch, or under a sink, when you're sixty years old? Not many. Your back is hurting, your knees are shot, you're fighting dehydration, and overheating every day. This is a young person's job. Most people in our industry spend the first five years getting into and learning the trade and the next thirty trying to get out of it. It's a tough gig.

These young people, mostly millennials, value time as much as, or more than, money. Coaching their kid's soccer team, taking weekends off, travelling, getting immersed in hobbies, sports, hunting, fishing, and being with their families . . . these are all things that take time, and they want as much of that as they can get. Companies need to think of *time* as a benefit, and examine how to provide employees more time to do the things important to them. Do that and your retention will improve.

No matter what business you're in, make sure you *win the war for talent.*

⛏ Pulling Back the Curtain

★   "You're only as good as your worst employee." You've heard the phrase. I'm don't believe that, but the point of the phrase does have some merit. In the war for talent, you must find what it is that attracts the best people in your industry because they will be the face of your company to the customer.

★   Everyone needs something and everyone wants something. Companies tend to focus on what their employees need (pay, benefits, security, etc.). If you want the best talent in your industry, also focus on what the talent wants. What do they want, what do they lack, what is their dream? *"To understand the heart and mind of a person, look not at what he/she has achieved already, but at what he/she aspires to."* —Kahlil Gibran

★   *"To win in the marketplace, you must first win in the workplace."* —Doug Conant

My Seventh Trick

Measuring Customer Satisfaction: A New Magical Scoring System

People don't buy goods and services. They buy relations, stories and magic.
—Seth Godin

LARGER COMPANIES ROUTINELY SPEND A LOT OF MONEY TO MEASURE CUSTOMER SATISFACTION. It is imperative, for *any* business, to have a good gauge of how customers view their service, their pricing and value, speed, etc. These can be measured several ways, but usually via satisfaction surveys. Voice of the Customer (VoC) and customer satisfaction scores are measured, used internally, and sometimes even advertised to give consumers comfort in what their experience will be. Here are two examples of common tools that companies use to measure customer satisfaction.

NPS – Net Promoter Score

This is one of the best measures of customer satisfaction. It's normally anchored in the question *How likely are you recommend our business to a friend or family member?* The scale is one to ten, with ten being most likely. You then subtract the percentage of zero-to-six scores (detractors) from the percentage of nine-to-ten scores (promoters) to arrive at a final score. Scores of seven and eight are considered *passive*. The scale is negative one hundred to positive one hundred. You are looking for a score above zero, with anything over fifty being exceptional.

OSAT - Overall Satisfaction

This is a basic measurement that's often used in advertising. It can be gamed a bit by how the question is asked and when you ask it (at the beginning of the survey or at the end), but it, too, is insightful. It normally might be based on the question *What was your overall satisfaction with the experience?* again based on a scale of one to ten. Some base it on a scale of *Extremely Satisfied, Very Satisfied, Satisfied, Neutral, Dissatisfied, Very Dissatisfied, Extremely Dissatisfied.* You can then measure the percent of the top two or top three in that range. A good indicator, but again it's hard to compare apples to apples between companies because of the variations in measurement and design. And a ninety-five-percent customer satisfaction rating seems like a powerful statement unless you're one of the five percent that wasn't satisfied.

There are many other customer-satisfaction scoring methods, including *Customer Effort Score, Customer Churn Rate, Customer Referrals,* and many others. Customer referrals are a great barometer but are often hard to measure accurately. In the service industry, there is one measurement that we watch that you don't often hear about. It's the litmus test of how good your service is. It's also the ultimate compliment anyone can give. That measurement is . . .

When the customer asks for you by name the next time they want service, you probably *wowed* **them the first time.**

Isn't that really the best compliment you can get? Isn't that a stamp of approval for trust and satisfaction? My wife and I frequent some restaurants and we always ask for the waiter or waitress by name. I always ask for my doctor by name versus getting one within a pool. When we go to the pet groomers, there is one groomer who is better with our dog than the others. We want her! When my wife goes to the stylist, nail salon, massage studio, you name it, she always asks for who she wants by name. Welcome to the easiest scoring system of customer satisfaction there is . . . and also the most effective.

> What happens when customers ask for you, or someone who works for you, by name?

- What you recommend is golden because they trust you.
- They tell others about you: more referrals.
- When overall business is slow you won't be.
- Many customers prefer to wait for someone they trust versus getting someone new. I've seen people wait a day or two, without hot water or AC, just to get a specific tech.
- You sell more, have higher tickets, get more tips, etc.
- You have leverage over your boss. They won't want you to leave when so many of their customers want you.

The job of any service professional, no matter what business you're in, is to get customers to ask for you by name. In the AC, plumbing, and electrical business, the average consumer often needs your service only once every two or three years unless they have a maintenance agreement. The repeat buying cycle is pretty spread out, so it's more difficult to develop a relationship in which they want to ask for a tech by name, or would even *remember* their name. To overcome this we teach our technicians the following:

1. **WOW them.** I won't get into *how* to WOW them, there are lots of books and seminars that focus on that, but giving the kind of

service a customer just can't help but tell someone about (in a good way), is what you're after.

Our HVAC installers are some of the hardest-working people in the world. It's a tough job. They're working in hot attics, on roofs, taking big systems out of small scuttle holes, crawling around in your attic for hours. The install is pristine, they do great work, and the customer is cool when they leave. Customers don't talk about that though. They paid for that. They expected that. What they talk about is how we wore shoe covers, laid down tarps to protect their flooring, were on the roof and stopped what we were doing to help the homeowner carry in the groceries, changed the batteries in their smoke detectors while they had the ladders out. These, and other things, are the WOWs and what they tell their neighbors about. Creating the kind of WOW experience you hear about comes down to doing things the customer didn't expect.

2. **Let them know they can ask for you by name.** Seems rudimentary, but when you say *If you liked the service I provided, next time you can ask for me by name* plants the seed. You can even add that since you're now familiar with their equipment, system, likes/dislikes, etc., you'll make sure they're well taken care of in the future. It's good to let them know how much it means to you when they ask for you by name. *Do me a favor* is a powerful way to start any ask. And *It would really mean a lot to me* is a great way to end it.

3. **Leave clues.**

a. Give them your business card, with your picture and name, and a referral offer on the back. Give them a few more to pass out to friends. What's the worst that can happen? They'll throw them away. They aren't doing any good sitting in your drawer at home anyway, so hand them out. What's the best that can happen? You'll get new business from new customers. Hand out ten or more each day. You'll be amazed by how it pays off.

b. If your business is performed inside people's homes, leave clues. We place stickers with our company name, services, and contact info on the systems that we service. Write your name on the stickers: *Ask for Paul Kelly—Thanks!* We sticker up the AC unit, the water heater, the disposal, the softener, RO drinking-water system, thermostat, inside the electrical panel, anything we service. When our techs sticker up the house, the house becomes our customer too, and anyone moving in later knows whom to call.

c. Write legibly on the invoice or receipt. At a lot of restaurants, the server writes their name, a thank you, and a smiley face on the receipt. It's a little gesture, but a nice touch.

If all else fails, let them know that if they don't remember your name, they can ask the CSR to send whomever they sent last time. Most companies can look it up.

 We can look in our system, run reports, or just run daily counts of how many calls are associated with specific techs, signifying the customer asked for them by name. For some techs, it's most of what they run each day. When they visit those customers, sometimes they get to know all about them, their favorite sports teams, where they grew up, their kids, their pets, what was going on in their lives during the last visit . . . maybe a sickness, maybe a marriage, maybe grandchildren. And our tech is familiar with their home, its plumbing, HVAC system, electrical system. It becomes family to our tech and the tech becomes family to our customer. Some customers will fix them dessert, have a cold lemonade ready, or look forward to updating them on what's going on in their lives.

So now you know the trick to measuring and creating greater customer satisfaction, securing repeat customers, and creating more referrals for you and your company. WOW your customers enough that they ask for you by name. Ask them to request you and leave clues to help them remember.

Do your customers say *OW!* or *WOW!?*

Ta-daaah!!!!!!

Pulling Back the Curtain

★　　WOWing a customer is all about doing things they didn't expect. Finding something you can do—without charging them for it— is something I learned from Vince, my old partner. There's always something, even if it's a just a little thing, that you can do to add value and show them you care.

★　　Once in a great while we can get an unreasonable customer. Regardless of what you may have heard, the customer *isn't* always right. But the customer *is* always the customer, and no matter what, our job is to make them happy. If you can get good at pleasing the most difficult customers you will totally WOW the vast majority of them who aren't.

Chapter Fifteen

⑨he ℘ower of ℘roximity: ⑤urround ⑥ourself ℳith ⑨alent

You become like the five people you spend the most time with.
Choose carefully.
—**Jim Rohn**

A BIG PART OF YOUR SUCCESS, in business and in life, is who you surround yourself with. No one does it alone. If you want to be a successful businessperson, then find some successful businesspeople and find ways to be around them (civic associations and chambers of commerce are great places to meet your new best friends). If you want to be a better parent, join a parenting group and start hanging out with great parents. On the other hand, if you want to be an underachiever, go hang out with low performers, lazy people, or excuse-makers. It works both ways. Be intentional about your circle of associates. Think carefully and choose wisely.

This chapter is about those who had the most influence on my life, those who have helped lead me to many successes and *Ta-daaah* moments. *Ta-daaahs* are meant to be shared. As you read this, ask yourself who has created *Ta-daaah* moments in *your* life, then write them down, along with how they influenced you, just like I did in the next few paragraphs.

We talked about my mom and dad. We talked about my wife's mom and dad as well. My brothers and sisters, Cathy, Sheila, Beth,

Ernie, Greg, John, and Jim all influenced me in different ways to become better at what I do and who I am. I can find a teacher and learn from them without the teacher ever knowing I'm being taught. I'm good at observing and learning from the best, even if sometimes from afar. My siblings are certainly teachers to me.

Josh, my son, and Justine, my daughter, are both mentioned in this book, and they've made me better in many ways. Their spouses, Laura and Pat, have also influenced me, sometimes through how they elevate Josh and Justine, but it's oftentimes by how they make me feel when I'm with them. *All four make me want to be the very best version of myself.* I have so many stories of how each has made me proud over the years and added to the success of our company.

I've mentioned Trisha, my wife, many times. She's been a big influencer in my life. She sacrificed much to move a handful of times to support my career and my dreams. She was the primary reason our kids turned out so well while I traveled during much of my early career. And she's worked with me in our business for the last ten years and more. I thought I worked hard—and I do—but she reminds me there's always more to give. She's one of the hardest working people I know.

We like to bounce ideas off of each other, and she keeps me grounded. She oversees the warehouse at our company, the fleet, building maintenance, security, office supplies and equipment, and plans and executes our company parties, recognitions, birthday cards (all hand-written), and so much more. On top of that, she oversees MyGuy Referrals, a referral company we jointly own. If her plate isn't full I don't know whose is. We occasionally have our ups and downs, and I won't say we never disagree about things, but I *will* say that we never fight about it. She's helped drive our success and I enjoy working with her. And like I tell her every morning as we drive to work,

"I sure am glad you come to work with me each day." She always responds, "I know. You need me so you can drive in the carpool lane." I just smile.

One of the biggest blessings that happened to our business was being able to land a gentleman named Daryl. Daryl was working for our biggest competitor, George Brazil. George was a pioneer in our industry and someone I learned from, even though he never knew it. I watched what he did, how he went to market, and how he changed our industry. George died in 2012. Without getting into the details, Daryl ended up approaching me the next year wanting to start up an electrical department for Parker & Sons. Although intrigued by starting electrical, I knew Daryl well and I wanted to see what other things Daryl could help me with first. As I told him, it's not *if* I'm going to hire you; you're hired. I just need to figure out *what* I'm going to do with you when you get here. Then and now, I had greater aspirations than just starting electrical.

Daryl has grown into one of the best leaders in our industry and he's a big reason we're now able to grow over twenty million dollars a year for the last four years. He and I work well together, and we have fun doing it. He has a unique way of looking at problems and boiling them down to something simple—sometimes so simple I get tickled about it. He's one of the better thinkers in our industry and he's now the president of our company. He's made me better and I think I've been able to do the same for him. If you're lucky enough to have a good right-hand person in your business, you know how valuable that can be.

There have been so many others who have influenced me over the years and who continue to do so. Some are old bosses and co-workers, some are new bosses and co-workers, some are friends, others are trainers, teachers, and mentors, and certainly many were and are other business leaders . . . and some even competitors. This chapter would never do them justice and the list is too long to thank them all, but I've been lucky to have learned from some of the best.

Our company has their unfair share of outstanding leaders, managers, supervisors, office workers, warehouse staff, salespeople, mechanics, and field-team members. We are truly blessed with some of the best in the industry, all right here in one company. We seem to attract them and it's fun to watch the company accelerate because of them.

If your business is lucky enough, your marriage lucky enough, or your family lucky enough, you end up surrounding yourself with people who take you to a whole other level as a leader, a spouse, a parent, a family member, or a friend. Trisha, Josh, Justine, our extended families, our friends, Daryl, others at work, and countless others I've met have all done that for me. I'm their *Ta-daaah*. That's quite the trick they all pull off, making me look good. I'm not sure how they do it, but like all magic, it's better I just enjoy it rather than try to figure it out.

Ta-daaah!!!

Pulling Back the Curtain

★ Did your parents worry about who you hung around with? Mine did. Friends will tell you a lot about who you become. Even some of the best parents can't influence their children enough to overcome "hanging with the wrong crowd" as my mom used to say.

★ *If you hang out with chickens, you're going to cluck, and if you hang out with eagles, you're going to fly* —Steve Maraboli

Chapter Sixteen

Enjoying Your Ta-daaahs

If you're not enjoying the journey, you probably won't enjoy the destination.
—**Robin Liefeld**

WE STARTED THIS BOOK talking about and defining *ta-daaah* moments, how to create more of them, and how to be more successful in your business, your job, and in life. I'd like to end this book with how to recognize **Ta-daaah** moments and, more importantly, *how to enjoy them.*

Ta-daaah moments are defined by you. You decide what is exceptional. It's your choice when, how, and with whom to celebrate something truly extraordinary. Some of these moments will be obvious: your wedding day, closing on a new house, the birth of a son or daughter, your thirtieth wedding anniversary, a new car, the first adventure on your new speed boat, a bucket-list vacation or event, completing your first marathon or some other big achievement, a record year in your business, closing a big account, celebrating an extraordinary month, an award your company achieved, a promotion, the corner office, or moving into the Mac Daddy of all cubicles.

Some *Ta-daaah* moments are less grandiose, yet still need to be celebrated and cherished. Your son learning how to swim or winning a wrestling match, your daughter's dance recital or her A in math, your wife's fiftieth birthday party or her being recognized in the local community. Some are not *your Ta-daaahs,* but simply those you're enjoying or celebrating with someone else, like your grandma's eightieth birthday or your boss's promotion.

And if you look hard enough, you'll begin to see *Ta-daaahs* in much of what you do or see in others. It could be as simple as an exquisite meal. Thanksgiving is like that to me because Trisha makes turkey and dressing to die for. And the gravy . . . oh my gosh . . . I think her gravy's a beverage. It's a *Ta-daaah* for sure.

Firsts are often *Ta-daaahs:* your child's first smile, first words, first step, first day of school, first competition, the lists go on and on. Pets have many *Ta-daaah* moments too, sometimes without little Buddy, Butler, Brody, Bookers, and Murphy knowing it (I told all our kids' dogs I'd work them into this book).

At work, there are *Ta-daaah* moments that you need to look out for and celebrate more often. It's an area I always have to work on myself: *recognizing the achievements of others.* We all get busy and forget to recognize the outstanding achievements that happen every day. At our company, we recognize all customer satisfaction letters, emails, calls, and texts. We seem to get a few every day; it's neat to read some of the outstanding things our employees do. Anything done extremely well can be a *Ta-daaah,* even turning an upset customer around to loving us once again. Our call center, dispatch team, field staff, and management staff do this every day by delighting our customers. An outstanding month or a big sale is certainly an achievement worth recognizing and celebrating.

By now, with all the examples used so far, and knowing I've only scratched the surface, you're probably realizing that a lifetime can contain thousands, maybe tens of thousands, of *Ta-daaahs* that you generate, that you are a part of generating, or that someone else has generated, that you get to celebrate. With so many, it's overwhelming to imagine how to celebrate them all. That's probably why we only celebrate the big ones. We seem to bottle up all that excitement and let it loose at a single celebration, like that retirement party at work, or your best friend's bachelor party (maybe *Ta-daaahing* a bit too much).

I want you to take a different approach. I'm going to challenge you and myself (because I'm still working on it) to appreciate more *Ta-daaah* moments, and because you are, to sometimes celebrate them a little less intensely. Does that sound like a contradiction? I'm not talking about the *big Ta-daaahs.* Celebrate those long and hard. Don't let anyone out-celebrate you! My family and extended family are great at this part. But beyond the big moments or occasions, start noticing the smaller wins, the less-obvious *Ta-daaahs,* and enjoy them, too. And find those moments in what others do, and let them know how special that moment, effort, performance, or unselfish act is.

 When you celebrate it, share it . . . with your loved ones, family, friends, co-workers, vendors, and other business partners. It's not just giving someone recognition, but making sure others recognize it too. Public recognition is powerful. It doesn't need to be a day-long party or a company outing or donuts for everyone, although chocolate eclairs *are* a great way to celebrate. It can be simple celebrations like these:

For yourself

- Buy yourself a massage or manicure
- Treat yourself to that chocolate malt
- Take a long walk with your dog
- Take a quick fifteen-nap to rejuvenate
- Shop for something for yourself
- Take yourself on a date to a nice restaurant
- Have a glass of wine

For a loved one

- Send flowers
- Mail a thank-you card
- Call someone you haven't talk to in a while and tell them how much they mean to you
- Take them to lunch or have it brought in
- Buy them a cute stuffed animal
- Have their house professionally cleaned

For someone at work

- Dinner for two at a restaurant of their choice
- A simple thank you, in person, or via text or email
- Buy pizza for the office
- Have their car detailed
- Feature them in the company newsletter
- Let them take half the day off

You get the idea. There are hundreds of small gestures and ways to celebrate that are inexpensive but still mean a lot. Be generous with recognizing, rewarding, and celebrating small ***Ta-daaahs.*** If you're having trouble identifying these moments or efforts, set a goal of recognizing and celebrating five or ten of these a day, including one or two of your own. Force yourself to celebrate. It's worth the effort.

🕴 Pulling Back the Curtain

★ Celebrating successes or something good that happens is something we can all do more. You've but one chapter left and an ending trick, and you'll have finished this book. Take a minute right now to celebrate. Do it now! You deserve it.

★ Go ahead, I'm waiting . . .

Chapter Seventeen

There's Magic in What You Think and Say

What you think, you become. What you feel, you attract. What you imagine, you create.
—**Buddha**

THERE IS A WORD THAT ENCAPSULATES THIS BOOK'S PRIMARY MESSAGE:

__Abracadabra__—an incantation used as a magic word in stage magic tricks, and historically was believed to have healing powers when inscribed on an amulet. —Wikipedia

Abracadabra is an old magic word which is used by very few magicians today. It's normally said just prior to transforming an object or at the climactic moment of an illusion. There's something mystical happening when the word is spoken, even if it isn't within a magical setting. I've heard people say abracadabra to communicate their power to change or improve something, e.g., "The company was losing money and we implemented the principles in Paul's book and *abracadabra*, we were making money in no time." ☺

But the word has a greater meaning. And although the origin of the word is uncertain, many believe it originated from an old Aramaic word meaning *I create as I speak, or I say it and I create it.*

I say it and I create it!

What a great mantra. You can say it out loud or you can say it to yourself. Visualization of an outcome is a technique often used in sports, but it can be used for anything you can think of. A pro golfer lines up the putt, stands over the ball, and visualizes the grain of the green, the break, the speed, the take back of the putter, the follow-through, and the ball rolling into the hole. He or she says to themselves, "I'm going to make this putt," and creates the action in their head. Visualization in sports is a powerful skill that most successful athletes use to one extent or another. I've played with less-skilled golfers who also use visualization, talking themselves into missing even the easiest of putts. Sometimes they silently say it to themselves and sometimes they say it out loud: "I know I'm going to miss this putt." "Yes, you will," I reply. You say it and you create it.

Now just because you've visualized it and said it doesn't mean it will happen every time, but if you get good at visualization your success rate will increase substantially. It's because, as you visualize, you start to *practice* that visualization. And we all know that practice makes perfect. Perfect practice, the skill of practicing what you visualize, exactly as you visualize it, makes for better outcomes.

I've played golf since I was a teenager. I was always decent, with a handicap in the twelve to sixteen range, depending on the course and how often I was playing. In laymen's terms, for all you non-golfers, I was slightly better than a bogey golfer. Don't know what a bogey golfer is? Okay, okay . . . I was better than average.

About ten years ago I decided to go to the driving range and not leave until I figured out how to draw a ball consistently, how to hit it straight consistently, how to slice it, and how to know and feel the difference. Most average golfers hit a bucket of balls at the driving range with no purpose other than to hit some balls. I was going there with a clear purpose, determined not to quit until I accomplished it. I say it and I create it.

Three buckets of balls later, with knowledge I had read in *Golf Digest* and online, and a lot of swings of the club, I had accomplished my goal. I could draw the ball on command, hit it straight, or revert back to my slice, and I could do it consistently. I could control my shots, something I hadn't been able to do before. I played a round of golf just three days later. It was one of the best rounds of my life. I ended up shooting a seventy-nine, seven over par. I broke the eighty mark, something I had done only once before, on a much easier course. I had shaved about seven strokes off my score and I didn't really even putt that well (because I hadn't practiced it perfectly). Not a golf person? That's okay. It will work for just about anything. I say it and I create it.

What you say (and do) to others, and to yourself, becomes your reality. In business, budgets are a way of saying what you're going to do and then creating that reality. Your company's vision, mission statement, or set of values, written down and hanging on the wall for everyone to see, says to each employee, *This is who we want to be and will become.* Writing down personal goals and keeping them in front of you, working each day on achieving them, is a way to say it and create it. Just like trying to remember someone's name, saying a worthwhile ideal or goal often enough helps you remember it. And remembering it keeps it top of mind, which then leads to achieving it. I say it . . . and I create it!

Abracadabra!!!!!

🕴 Pulling Back the Curtain

★   Abracadabra!

★   Hocus pocus!

★   Shazam!

★   Alakazam!

★   Open sesame!

★   Presto chango!

★   Voilà!

★   À la peanut butter sandwiches!

★   Whatever your magic word or phrase of choice, just know that there is magic in thoughts, words, deeds, and actions. What you create in life or business will be the sum of what you say, what you think, and what you do. It will become your body of work, built throughout your life. Let that body of work be something you are proud of. The lesson is evident throughout *The Bible,* the greatest book ever written: *What you sow, so shall you reap.*

My Final Trick

... *In This Book*

AS WITH ANY PERFORMANCE, the ending or finale is what creates the lasting impression. I hope you enjoyed this book. I know I enjoyed writing it.

I hope your life, business, or job is full of *Ta-daaah* moments and that you learn to recognize and celebrate them. I hope this book gave you some insight into how to be more successful and create more of these precious moments for yourself, your loved ones, and others.

I'll leave you with my final trick. Pull out your phone and use your calculator, or use a pencil and paper.

1.   Pick any three-digit number, as long as the same number never repeats. Write it here _____

2.   Reverse that three-digit number, with the last digit first and the first digit last _____

3.   Subtract the smaller three-digit number from the larger number and write the difference _____

4.   Now reverse the three digits of the number in step three

_____

5.   Add the numbers in steps three and four _____

6.   Take the first three digits of that number and go to that page in this book. Take the fourth digit of that same number in step five and count to that word in the first paragraph.

And there is your . . . ***Ta-daaah!!!!!!!***

Appendix

The PK Rotational Diet

THIS DIET WORKS, based on my own experience and the experiences of others. However, as always, please check with your doctor before beginning this or any other dietary or weight-loss program. I can't be held responsible if things go wrong!

Got your permission slip? Okay, here it is:

The PK Rotational Diet

Day 1 – All Liquids. Drink plenty of fluids, mostly water, but nothing caloric. No food. This is your toughest day. Fight through it, for tomorrow you will eat.

Day 2 – All Vegetables. No potatoes or heavy starches, but everything else is fair game, cooked or raw. Broccoli, cauliflower, beans, spinach, celery, cucumbers, etc. Eat regular portions, but don't overindulge.

Day 3 – All Fruits. Have at it: apples, oranges, bananas, melons, berries. Again, don't overindulge, but do eat to be full.

Day 4 – Atkins. Low or (preferably) no carbs. You know the drill.

Day 5 – Salad. Light dressing is okay, even some light cheese, tomatoes, cucumbers, etc. You're going to play rabbit for a day.

Day 6 – Cheat Night. If you started your diet on Monday, this day would be Saturday. It's a light lunch, like a salmon Caesar salad, and then for dinner it's cheat night. Have whatever you want, except for bread, potatoes, fries, and other starches.

Day 7 – Breakfast. An omelet with whatever you want in it, or eggs, bacon, and sausage. No pancakes or toast or potatoes though.

A small salad for lunch, or skip it. And salad with chicken or fish for dinner.

Alcohol is off limits for this week, except maybe on cheat night when you can have one or two. Drink lots of water and low/no calorie drinks.

Weigh in before you start. Weigh in every day during the diet. I sometimes weigh in twice a day just to see how I'm doing. Like any goal, the more often you measure how you're doing, the better you tend to do. I get a kick out of weighing in before I go to bed and then when I wake up. Sometimes I'll lose a pound overnight. I've occasionally lost two. Psychologically, losing weight while sleeping is very gratifying. I can't wait to get to go to sleep knowing I'm losing weight doing it 😊. Weighing in every day, especially after you lose your weight, is critical. If you gain a pound or two back, you'll know it right away and can do something that day to lose it again. But if you weigh in once a week or once a month, you may be surprised to learn you've gained all the weight back and more. Yo-yo diets are never good for the mind, much less the body. Weighing in daily will help you prevent that.

I can lose seven to eight pounds in a week on the PK Rotational Diet, which is mostly how long I stay on it. I have done it for two weeks and lost twelve pounds. My kids have tried it; so have my siblings and several friends and it seems to work. Most lose six or seven pounds in a week; one lost ten. Nice!

My son Josh asked, "What's the science behind why it works?" I said, if you eat one type of food, without other things with it, your body can process it more easily and you'll eat less, too. He asked, "How do you know that?" I answered, like I do sometimes at work, "I don't know for sure, but that's my theory. All I know for sure is that it works." He just laughs. "So this is a diet plan, not based on any science you know of, and you just made it up?" I say "Yep, you got it." ***Ta-daaah!***

About Paul Kelly

PAUL KELLY'S UNIQUE BACKGROUND and simplified approach to growing a business has led him to be one of the most successful leaders in the home-services industry. His specialty is taking something complicated and reducing it to something very simple, making it easier to implement. Drawing on lessons learned since childhood, he has found a winning formula for succeeding at life and business at their highest levels.

Paul has over thirty-five years of experience in the home-services industry and has held prominent positions in finance, sales, marketing, and operations for national and regional companies. He has helped over a hundred of America's best service companies improve revenue and profits. In 2004 he bought Parker & Sons, a Phoenix HVAC and plumbing company, and grew it from a small company with twenty-five trucks and seven million dollars in annual revenue to over four hundred trucks and a 2021 run rate approaching two hundred million dollars, the largest of its kind in America.

Family is important to Paul, as is sharing his *Tricks of the Trade to Success,* just as others have done with him. Sharing his knowledge, experience, fortune, and fun is the magic he enjoys most.

YOU'RE STILL HERE??

THE BOOK WASN'T ENOUGH? YOU WANT MORE?

Although busy with growing his business in Phoenix, and additional duties as the Wrench Group's Southwestern CEO, Paul is available for speaking engagements or group consulting on a limited basis. He hopes to expand his ability to help other businesses and organizations as he works his way to semi-retirement in the next year or two or three ☺.

If you are a best-in-class contractor in the HVAC, plumbing, or electrical business wishing to prepare your business for sale, he can also help you with that. The Wrench Group is always interested in elite contractors with a history of growth and profitability in various markets.

Visit Paul's website for details and contact information.

www.TricksOfTheTrade.com